T0147253

A Smoother Transition

Why Teenagers Make Rational and Irrational Choices

By

Ella L. Johnson, PH.D
&
Dianne E. Barber, PH.D

iUniverse, Inc.
New York   Bloomington

A Smoother Transition
Why Teenagers Make Rational and Irrational Choices

The views expressed in this work are solely those of the author
and do not necessarily reflect the views of the publisher, and
the publisher hereby disclaims any responsibility for them.
iUniverse books may be ordered through booksellers or by contacting:

iUniverse
1663 Liberty Drive
Bloomington, IN 47403
www.iuniverse.com
1-800-Authors (1-800-288-4677)

Because of the dynamic nature of the Internet, any Web addresses or
links contained in this book may have changed since publication and may
no longer be valid. The views expressed in this work are solely those of
the author and do not necessarily reflect the views of the publisher, and
the publisher hereby disclaims any responsibility for them.

ISBN: 978-1-4401-1661-2 (pbk)
ISBN: 978-1-4401-1662-9 (ebk)

Printed in the United States of America

iUniverse rev. date: 1/27/2009

Disclaimer

The authors and publisher of this book have put forth their best efforts in preparing this material. The information contained in the book is for educational purposes. Therefore, if you wish to apply ideas contained in this book, you are taking full responsibility for your actions. The authors, publisher, editor or distributors shall in no event be held liable to any party for the direct, indirect, punitive, special, incidental or other consequential damage arising directly from any use of this book. The goal is to provide you with educational information that may be useful in attaining a better understanding of the teenage experience. Nothing in it is meant as counseling, psychology, psychiatric or as medical advice. Teenagers you should get the consent of your parents, or those in authority before implementing any changes, especially if you have physical problems or are taking medications of any kind.

Dedication

This book is dedicated to teens everywhere. Here's to who you are now and who you choose to become.

Acknowledgement

It is with love and appreciation that we acknowledge and give thanks to our family: Our parents, Mr. & Mrs. Andrew Lee Matthews, who instilled in us high moral values and taught us to carry ourselves with dignity and respect. We are so appreciative and grateful to our dad (who passed away), for working so hard to give us a better life, and for encouraging us to pursue a higher education: To Our darling mother for her unconditional love, support, and encouraging us to pursue our interests. Our daughters: Rolanda Faulks, Andrea Thomas, Almetta Garner, and Lanita Wilson, (who passed away at the age of thirty-two) for believing in us, and encouraging us to pursue our dreams. They had confidence in us when we doubted ourselves, and brought out the good ideas in us. Without their encouragement and moral support we could not have finished this book. To Kyara and Brandon Wilson, thank you for being so patient and helpful. We love you more than you'll ever know.

We are indebted to our brother, Dr. Elder Fred Matthews, Sr. our sisters: Dr. Daisy Gaitors, Ms. Annette Smith, and Ms. Jacqueline Matthews for their inspiration, for never accepting anything less than our best efforts, for always being there to listen and give encouraging words of wisdom, and mainly for being such perfect role models. We give special thanks to our sister, Dr. Delores Livingston who is most responsible for helping us complete the writing of this book as well as the challenging research that lies behind it. She encouraged and motivated us and provided inspirational resources. With lots of patience, she showed us different ways to approach a research problem and the need to be persistent to accomplish any goal. Our siblings are more than brother and sisters; they are our closest friends.

Abstract

Adolescence is time for growth and development, and teenager's brains are changing so much. Adolescence is a time of fun, adventure, and socializing. Yet, today's youth are also under tremendous pressure, often experimenting with tobacco, alcohol, illicit drugs, and sex.

Teenagers today are far more vulnerable than in past generations. Our society is changing, as a result many taboos and stigmas of the past have been removed. We see a decline in values and a break down in family structures. We also see a lack of respect for authority figures which affect teen behavior and viewpoints.

Teens face many more problems than their parents or grandparents. This is causing problems for parents because they want to rear children the way they were reared, and some of the old child-rearing methods are ineffective for today's adolescents. New gadgets and technological advances have exposed adolescence to a lot more than their parents and grandparents.

Some areas of the adolescent mind are undeveloped, yet many adolescents are trying to make adult decision in a child's brain. Teens often believe that they are invincible and some of devastating results can occur when they take risks without fully considering the consequences.

The purpose of this research is to bring public awareness of what adolescence experience. It is also crucial for parents and society in general to understand the impact of the under developed teenage mind and how it affects rational and irrational decision.

Table of Contents

Preface

For some parents, the terrible twos are nothing compared to the terrible teens. Of all the phases of human development, adolescence is probably the most challenging and it becomes fascinating once you understand the changes the teenage brain goes through.

This book explores the adolescent mind from three perspectives: What scientists have discovered; how parents and society can help during this stage of teenage life, and what teenagers want.

The first chapter provides the reader with an orientation to the study of adolescent growth and development including stages of puberty. Chapter 2 provides research into the developing teen brain. Chapter 3 discusses the risky behavior of teenagers, placing emphasis on teen suicide, HIV/AIDS, and teenage pregnancy. Chapters 4, 5, and 6 explore how teens make the transition into early adulthood. These chapters consider the under developed brain and its impact on dating abuse, abusive relationships, recognizing signs of low self-esteem, and some fears of teenagers. Chapter 7 is devoted to interacting and communicating with adolescents. It describes what teens and parents want and how parents can help teens through this period of stress and turmoil, Chapter 8 lists teen favorites.

Understanding how the development of the teenage mind affects rational and irrational decisions is important and should be read by parents, teachers, church and youth leaders in order to help teens during this stage of their lives to make an easier transition into adulthood.

Introduction

Adolescents today are a lot different than adolescents of yesterday. In generations past, our grandparents and great grandparents married as early as age 14 and were raised more family oriented. Society viewed marriage as permanent and if a couple got divorced there was a stigma attached. Divorce was frowned upon so couples generally stayed together and there were very few failed marriages. Children were prepared for their roles in the family; boys were taught a trade in order to be providers and girls were taught domestic skills and child rearing. Teenagers knew their place and were very respectful. Adolescent life skills that were taught in the past are not being taught as much to adolescents today. Many are latch key children and in some homes the television is being used as a babysitter. In addition, our society has changed as well as the make-up of the family. We're a mobile society now with increased technological advances. Many children are now being reared by grandparents, single parents, foster parents, stepparents, and same sex couples. Some adolescents have incarcerated parents or family members while others have extended families living in different states. The rise in delinquency appears to be related in part to these changes in the structure of the family.

What are some of the underlying causes as to why adolescents are so different today than in past generations? One problem facing adolescents and society as a whole is the fact that morals, values and religious principles have changed, but God's Word concerning the family has remained the same. A lot of people seem to be hearers of God's Word but are no longer doers of the Word. Teaching family values in the home was once considered to be a major part of child rearing but is no longer given the same priorities. Other causes facing today's adolescents are that they are faced with so much more than their parents had to face. Teens today are exposed to severe social and environmental issues such as the pressure to use drugs and alcohol, live up to the expectations of their peers, and to have sex before marriage. A lot of today's adolescents are more rebellious, more troubled psychologically, more promiscuous, unrealistic, and more critical of the values and standards of adult culture. In contrast, some adolescents are brighter and smarter than teens in past generations, more idealistic, open, responsible, and less troubled by their sexual attitudes and beliefs. This vast difference in today's adolescents is presenting problems for modern day parents because they want to rear children the way they were reared, yet many child rearing techniques and laws concerning children have not remained the same. It used to be very uncommon for parents to have the police called on them for disciplining their children, now it is the norm. We are seeing a whole new era in child rearing.

According to various studies on the topic, the adolescent brain changes a lot. Science indicates that their brain is not fully developed and the area of the brain involved in planning and decision-making has not reached its full potential. While teens attempt to declare their independence by withdrawing from their family and turning to their peers for advice, they want to make their own choices, but in reality these adolescents need their parent's guidance the most. At this point in their lives some teens do not want to be told what to do, and simply hate to be questioned. What they do not realize is that they are trying to make grown-up decisions with an underdeveloped brain.

When people understand some of the basics of how the brain is changing, they tend to be a lot more patient with teens. Add hormones and family stress to this mix and you can start to realize what teens are up against. There are physical and emotional changes happening with teens, including sexual development. These changes are being undertaken by a brain that is incapable of functioning like an adult brain. If you ask an adolescent "Why did you do that?" They will almost always say, "I don't know," and maybe that's truer than we thought. Any time teens have to be questioned about how they feel, or their reasons for doing something, a lot of kids will think of it as a demand to know what they think and feel, and the teenager's response is, "Leave me alone, I don't want to talk about it." When teenagers tend to withdraw and ask to be left alone is exactly when it's most important to engage them. Parents must be both patient and persistent.

The neocortex (the part of the brain responsible for language, decision-making functions, empathy, and planning) hasn't fully developed in the average thirteen-year-old. That teenager still depends on a more reactive part of the brain, the amygdala, which handles emotions and memories associated with feelings. According to Sara Goudarzi LiveScience (Sept. 8, 2006), if you ever sense teenagers are not taking your feelings into account, it's probably because they're just incapable of doing so. The area of the brain associated with higher-level thinking, empathy, and guilt is underused by teenagers, reports a new study. When considering an action, the teenage medial prefrontal cortex, located in front of the brain, doesn't get as much action as adults.

CHAPTER 1

Stages of Adolescence

The word "adolescence" means a "period of growth to maturity." It begins at puberty (the beginning of the growth spurt and sexual maturation) and extends to the late teens or early twenties. Puberty is the stage of adolescence in which an individual becomes physiologically capable of sexual reproduction. Basically, it's moving from one stage of life to another. During this period, the individual's intellectual capacity completes its development, including concepts of logic and reasoning.

Teenage life consists of a multitude of emotional peaks and valleys, ranging from exhilarating highs to depressing lows. Adolescence is perceived by many as the period of becoming…. It is a time when identities are established, a time to remember first love, first date, and first kiss. The adolescent world is often confusing and changes so quickly that immature young people do not always adjust efficiently. This has led some to describe adolescence as a highly disruptive period characterized by rebellion, perpetual turmoil, and stormy periods of stress.

During this stage of life, the adolescent changes physically, emotionally, sexually, and intellectually while attempting to shift away from dependency and the restrictions of the family and to move toward independence and social effectiveness. Adolescents may become scornful with the beliefs of their parents and society; they either accept such values or find substitutes, thus the adolescent accepts some parental values, rejects others, or modifies them. Gradually the adolescent develops a personal value system.

Adolescents are often unable to break their early emotional bonds logically. They may become rebellious emotionally, or hypercritical in order to persuade their parents that they are now different and must be independent. This behavior may breed alienation (the generation gap). Sharing family time remains important and adolescents gain strength from the family even while they are actively seeking their independence.

Adolescence is a period of transitions; biological, psychological, social, and economic. It is an exciting time of life. Individuals become more interested in sex, and become biologically capable of having children. They become more sophisticated and attempt to make their own choices. It is the period following childhood, the period between childhood and adulthood. It is a transitional period where adolescents begins to take on more responsibility and is expected to become more responsible for their own choices and actions.

Teens are moving from immaturity to maturity. The stages of adolescence vary differently with each adolescent. During adolescence, so much psychological and social growth takes place that most Social Scientists feel it make more since to divide adolescence into three parts; early, middle and late adolescence. Early adolescent teens have little in common with a late teen; their interest and concerns are different. Biological changes of adolescents dramatically increase in height and body for both sexes. The height of boys before age 11 tend to be taller than girls before age 11; between ages 11 and 13 girls tend to be taller than boys. Boys catch up and tend to be taller than girls from age 14 onward. Between fifth and sixth grades you can see differences in height. Their height is a result of their upper body rather than in their leg length. Accelerated growth can be measured; the head, hands, and feet first, then accelerated growth in the arms and legs, later the torso and shoulder grow. Along with growth spurt in height comes an increase in body weight.

Stages of Puberty

Five Stages of Puberty - Guys

1. Normal Age Range: 9-12, Average: about 10

Male hormones are becoming active, but there are hardly, if any, outside signs of development. Testicles are maturing, and some boys start a period of rapid growth late in this stage.

2. Normal Age Range: 9-15, Average: 12-13

Testicles and scrotum begin to enlarge, but penis size doesn't increase much. Very little, if any, pubic hair is at the base of the penis. Increase in height and change in body shape.

3. Normal Age Range: 11-16, Average: 13-14

Penis starts to grow in length, but not much in width. Testicles and scrotum are still growing. Pubic hair starts to get darker and coarser and is spreading towards the legs. Height growth continues and body/face shape look more adult. Voice begins to deepen (and crack). Some hair around the anus grows.

4. Normal Age Range: 11-17, Average: 14-15

Penis width increases, as well as length. Testicles and scrotum are still growing. Pubic hair begins to take adult texture, although covers a smaller area. Most boys have first ejaculations. Underarm hair develops. Facial hair increases on chin and upper lip. Voice gets deeper and skin gets oilier.

5. Normal Age Range: 14-18, Average: around 16

Nearing full adult height and physique. Pubic hair and genitals have adult appearance. Facial hair grows more completely and shaving may begin now or soon.

During the late teens and early twenties, some men grow a bit more and develop more body hair, especially chest hair.

Five Stages of Puberty - Girls

1. Age Range: Usually 8-11

In Stage 1 there are no outside signs of development, but a girl's ovaries are enlarging and hormone production is beginning.

2. Age Range: Usually 8-14. Average: 11-12

The first sign is typically the beginning of breast growth, including "breast buds." A girl may also grow considerable height and weight. The first signs of pubic hair start out fine and straight, rather than curly.

3. Age Range: Usually 9-15. Average: 12-13

Breast growth continues, and pubic hair coarsens and becomes darker, but there still isn't a lot of it. Your body is still growing, and your vagina is enlarging and may begin to produce a clear or whitish discharge, which is a normal self-cleansing process. Some girls get their first menstrual periods late in this stage.

4. Age Range: Usually 10-16. Average: 13-14

Pubic hair growth takes on the triangular shape of adulthood, but doesn't quite cover the entire area. Underarm hair is likely to appear in this stage, as is menarche. Ovulation (release of egg cells) begins in some girls, but typically not in a regular monthly routine until Stage 5.

5. Age Range: Usually 12-19. Average: 15

This is the final stage of development, when a girl is physically an adult. Breast and pubic hair growth are complete, and your full height is usually attained by this point. Menstrual periods are well established, and ovulation occurs monthly.

During early adolescence (ages 11-14) peer networks will usually be teenagers of the same sex. Peer network is large group of peers with whom adolescents associate. This falls under three categories; best friends, cliques, and crowds. A clique is a group of peers who share similar values and beliefs – smaller in size than a crowd, but larger than a small group of friends. As an adolescent reach age 13, they distinctly view him/herself as an adolescent, having abandoned childlike behaviors. The 14 year old seeks peers who will support his/her ego ideals. They are interested in being accepted by others. During middle adolescence, ages 15-18 peer groups are usually teenagers in which male and females interact and are large peer groups. The 15 year old is outgrowing parental control and is attempting to break away from it. With the search for independence nearly over, the 16 year old self usually replaces rebellion with self-confidence, and serious thoughts of the future. During late adolescence 18-21 the large peer groups become smaller.

Storm and Stress

The assumption has been that teenage sturm and drang, (known as storm and stress) the insolence and the rages, are all directed at parents and authority figures, in an effort to define who they are and to assert their independence. The alternative explanation was that hormones, those glands that bring sexual stirrings and pimples, were to blame. The true source of teenage behavior lies north of the gonads. It's that 3 pound blob of gray and white matter known as the brain. Yes, teenagers do have brains, but theirs are under-developed and don't yet function like an adult's brain. With MRI, magnetic resonance imaging, neuroscientists have discovered that the adolescent brain is far from mature. "The teenage brain is a work in progress," says Sandra Witelson, a neuroscientist at McMaster University in Ontario.

CHAPTER 2

The Adolescent Brain

Brain Changes

The most surprising thing about the teen brain is how much it is changing. Parts of the brain undergo refinement during the teen years. Areas associated with more basic functions, including the motor and sensory areas, mature early. Areas involved in planning and decision-making, including the prefrontal cortex (the cognitive or reasoning area of the brain important for controlling impulses and emotions) appear not to have yet reached adult dimension during the early twenties.

The brain's reward center, the ventral striatum, also is more active during adolescence than in adulthood, and that region is a motivational center. It energizes action toward a goal. James Bjork, a neuroscientist at the National Institute on Alcohol Abuse and Alcoholism, states, "What we found is that the parts of the brain that are in the frontal lobe, that tend to assign picture value to rewards in the environment were the same in adolescents and adults. What was deficient in the adolescents is the circuitry at the base of the brain in a region called the ventral striatum, and that region is a motivational center. It energizes action toward a goal. And we found that that was markedly deficient in the adolescents." This could explain why it may be harder for some teens to get motivated. "Consider a person who has a motivational deficit," he says. "This kind of person would be drawn toward behaviors or activities that have either a very high reward or payoff factor or a very low effort factor because it's the same as saying 'What do I get out of this activity?' versus 'How much effort do I have to expend to get it?' One example of activities with really high reward-to-effort payoffs would be playing video games with their buddies, that they derive pleasure from was markedly deficient in adolescents. The adolescent brain still is strengthening connections between its reasoning- and emotion-related regions.

Another major finding is that game playing sometimes involves exposure to mature content, with almost a third of teens playing games that are listed as appropriate only for people older than they are.

Journal reference: *Journal of Neurosciences* (vol 24, p7) *Journal of Neuroscience* reveals that adolescent laziness may be determined by human biology. Researchers found that the section of the brain associated with drive and motivation, the right ventral striatum, is far less developed in teens than in adults. This explains the blank stares parents get when they ask a 13-year-old to throw out the garbage, or finish their book report. It could even explain why the 16-year-old could sleep past noon every day of the week. The teen brain requires a lot more stimulation before anything registers.

Teenagers and adults often don't see eye to eye, but new brain research is explaining why. Although adolescence is often characterized by increased independence and a desire for knowledge and exploration, it is also a time when brain changes can result in high-risk behaviors, addictions, and mental illness, as different parts of the brain mature at different rates.

As stated earlier, the most surprising thing about the teen brain is how much it is changing. By age six, the brain is already 95 percent of its adult size. But the gray matter, or thinking, part of the brain, continues to thicken throughout childhood as the brain cells get extra connections, much like a tree growing extra branches, twigs and roots. In the frontal part of the brain, the part of the brain involved in judgment, organization, planning, strategizing (those very skills that teens get better and better at) this process of thickening of the gray matter peaks at about age 11 in girls and age 12 in boys, roughly about the same time as puberty. After that peak, the gray matter thins as the excess connections are eliminated or pruned. So much of our research is focusing on trying to understand what influences or guides the building-up stage when the gray matter is growing extra branches and connections and what guides the thinning or pruning phase when the excess connections are eliminated.

The Difference between Adult & Child Brain

Scientists once thought the brain's key development ended within the first few years of life. Current findings indicate that important brain regions undergo refinement through adolescence and at least into a person's twenties. Scientists now can map brain tissue growth spurts and losses, allowing researchers to compare brain growth in both health and disease and to pinpoint where brain changes are most prominent in disease.

Many teens, for example, use adolescence as a time to experiment with drugs. A 2004 study found that 70 percent of high school seniors used alcohol in the previous year. What's more, the adolescent's brain may be particularly vulnerable to the negative effects of drugs, including becoming addicted later in life more so than people who don't use drugs before age 21.

Atypical brain changes and behaviors also can appear in adolescence. A 2005 report found that an estimated 2.7 million children and adolescents are reported by their parents to suffer from severe emotional or behavioral difficulties.

During adolescence, brain connections and signaling mechanisms selectively change over time to meet the needs of the environment. Overall, gray matter volume increases at earlier ages, followed by sustained loss and thinning starting around puberty, which correlates with advancing cognitive abilities. Scientists think this process reflects greater organization of the brain as it prunes redundant connections, and increases in myelin, which enhance transmission of brain messages.

Adults think with the prefrontal cortex. That's the rational portion of the brain.

Teens think with the amygdala. That's the instinctual and emotional portion of the brain.

Recent studies, such as the one done by NIH's Institute of Mental Health and UCLA's Laboratory of Neuro Imaging, show that many life changing decisions such as marriage and serving in the military are made before adolescent brains are fully ready to make such decisions.

Dr. Lauren Steinberg of Temple University studies teens and decision-making. He states that teen brains are different from adult brains. He said in an interview on CNN that the changes that take place in teen brains make teens want to take more risks and to seek higher and higher levels of stimulation.

Sometimes, stating the obvious helps. In this case, we think it does. Teenagers are not adults. Their bodies are different. So it turns out, are their minds. The fact that teens think differently explains a lot about why they don't act like adults, not in the classroom or at the mall, and certainly not when they get behind the wheel."

"They don't have the same kind of fear that adults do. Teens are different from adults for some really basic physiological decisions. Their brains are simply different. Source: CNN Newsnight

Making Rational Decisions

Rational decision making is a process for making logically sound decisions. After defining the problem, and thinking about all the possible alternatives, evaluate the options to anticipate the consequences. Rational decision is passing judgment on an issue. This is thinking before you act.

According to research done by neuroscientist Dr. Deborah Yurgelun-Todd, teenagers and adults process information and make judgments (decisions) using different parts of the brain. She and other colleagues at the McLean Hospital Brain Imaging Center in Boston, Massachusetts, discovered this using magnetic resonance imaging (MRI) to scan brains.

As a teenager moves into adulthood, there seems to be a shift in where the brain routes judgment calls, from the amygdalae (groups of neurons located deep within the medial temporal lobes) to the frontal lobe. That is, the brain transitions from making decisions from a more emotionally-based assessment of events to a more rationally-based approach. Throw into this mix the abuse of alcohol or illegal drugs, or risky behavior in general, and it becomes even more difficult for the adolescent or young adult mind to fully appreciate the consequences of some choices.

This is not to say that the youthful brain does not think rationally or that young people are not held accountable for their actions by God (Ecclesiastes 11:9). It is just that the brain is still going through development. Sometimes a teen's emotions get in the way of them making rational decisions. And sometimes they simply don't consider the consequences of certain choices, as shown by the seven binge-drinking college students who drowned in the Mississippi River and the hundreds of others who also died while abusing alcohol. This is where obedience to God's commands on not getting drunk offers an extra level of protection. The truth of the matter is God's way of life is always the best way of life for young and old.

Rational thinking is when people weigh the influences of motives and bias, and recognizes their own assumptions or point of view. They have the ability to reason. People are concerned more with finding the best explanation than being right or asking questions. They recognize emotional impulses, selfish motives, or other modes of self-deception.

Making Irrational Decisions

Irrationality is talking or acting without regard to what is sensible. Human brains are far more developed and elaborate in their frontal regions. During adolescence, these portions of the brain are heavily remolded and rewired, as teenagers learn (often excruciatingly slowly) how to exercise adult decision-making skills, like the ability to focus, to discriminate, to predict and to ponder questions of right and wrong.

Research shows that alcohol creates disruption in parts of the brain essential for self-control, motivation and goal setting and can compound pre-existing genetic and psychological vulnerabilities. Alcohol also appears to damage more severely the frontal areas of the adolescent brain, crucial for controlling impulses and thinking through consequences of intended actions, capacities many addicts and alcoholics of all ages lack. People fail to realize the irrationality of their actions and believe they are acting perfectly normal. Some teens have a tendency to view their actions as rational and to see those who disagree as irrational. Adolescents may be more willing to engage in dangerous activities such as drunk driving because the ventral striatum, this crucial part of their brain, is under-developed.

Risk-taking is much higher in teens than in adults. Teenagers are more likely to abuse drugs and alcohol and take sexual risks, but the reasons for it are hotly debated. Now researchers at the US National Institute on Alcohol Abuse and Alcoholism have found evidence for a difference in brain chemistry in a part of the brain involved in calculating risk and reward.

Journal reference: *Journal of Neurosciences* (vol 24, p7) *Journal of Neuroscience* reveals that adolescent laziness may be determined by human biology. Researchers found that the section of the brain associated with drive and motivation—the right ventral striatum—is far less developed in teens than in adults. This explains the blank stares parents get when they ask a 13-year-old to throw out the garbage, or finish their book report. It could even explain why the 16-year-old could sleep past noon every day of the week. The teen brain requires a lot more stimulation before anything registers.

- Do not make any serious decisions because you are angry, hurt, depressed, desperate, or frightened. Do not make decisions just to get revenge or to harm someone else. Do not make decision when you are incapable of rational thought. Make decisions for the right reasons and when you are calm and thoughtful. Even at these states of mind you must decide whether making any decision is necessary or desirable. Spend some careful thought before acting, so that you will not end up making unnecessary problems. Fears influence your decision making process.

Fear is disabling beliefs you carry in yourself that prevent you from living a productive, healthy, and growth-enhancing life. They are excuses behind which people hide to avoid change or growth. Fear is the underlying motive behind many of your actions and lack of action that block your thinking, problem solving and decision making abilities.

Fears come in a variety of packages for people who have low self-esteem, such as the fear of: Places, animals, objects, people, events, atmosphere, family member, disaster: reactions or responses to self: results of taking a risk to do something, public speaking, feelings about oneself, the unknown, and authority figures.

Fear can:

- Immobilize decision making.
- Prevent you from overcoming your insecurity, prevent you from trusting in others, and prevent you from being willing to become vulnerable in order to grow.
- Keep you locked in self-destructive behavior.
- Be the reason why you find yourself stuck in old ways of acting and believing.

What beliefs do people with an active fear-led life share?

- No matter what I do, I'll never be able to overcome that fear.
- Things are always going to be this way, so there is no use in trying.
- I'll never change. It is just a waste of time to try.

To overcome fear people need to:

- Identify the fear, label it, visualize it, and deal with it as if it were an object or entity to be remolded, changed, or altered. Be willing am I to try out new behavior
- Let go of insecurity, develop trust in themselves and others, and permit themselves to be vulnerable to change and growth.
- Stop or "turn off" obsessing thoughts about the feared objects or events.

CHAPTER 3

Transition – Early, Middle and Late Adolescence

Teen Experience

Adolescence is generally considered a time of conflict and growth. The teen changes physically, sexually, emotionally, intellectually, and socially. As they change from dependence and the family protective environment towards independence, life for many teens is filled with friendships, television, sports, school, study, socializing, phone, e-mail, and making plans together.

Teens are growing up so fast that with all the rapid changes they experience this often leads to a lot of stress and thinking about their lives, such as what's going on, what to do next, how to cope, who to trust, and who to turn to for support.

Teens will experience mood swings going between maturity and immaturity. They have a great desire to be accepted and have teenage language that they identify with. Dating and romance take on greater meaning. Relationship breakups are very painful.

Adolescence is a Time of Change

Prior to adolescence, young person may have accepted their parents standards with little question or challenge. The impact was families united and cooperating in common goals. Parental authority usually went unchallenged; parents molded and shaped the beliefs and values of their children. Today's teens, when there is confusion or feeling that they can't talk to their parents, often turn to equally confused and struggling peers for advice much to the distress of parents. Adolescents want a lot of freedom, but they handle it better when it is given in smaller and slowly increasing amounts.

- *Pre adolescence* is often divided into three overlapping time frames. Pre-adolescence or early adolescence begin around age ten or eleven and continues for a couple of years.

- *Middle adolescence* is the period from age 14 to 15 - during high school years.

- *Post adolescence* begins when high school ends. These challenges they will face as early causes them to move between maturity and immaturity.

- According to Dr. Gary Collins, Ph.D., author of Christian Counseling, adolescence 18-21 must answer questions: Who am I? It can be a time of self-searching, experimentation with lifestyles, anxiety, confusion, peer pressure, family expectations, concerns about the future, choosing a college, career, difficult choice for adolescents. Sometimes they are overly optimistic and unrealistic in career directions. This can lead to constant re-evaluation their choices. What Do I believe? Adolescents see and hear so much, so the question becomes what do I believe? In the process, teens are asking questions of society or blaming others, seeking self exploration and mini life adventure; teens eventually develop their own set of values.

Declaring Independence

Teenagers just finishing high school are so excited, and many teens have already been accepted into college and can't wait to get out on their own. Other teens are getting ready to get their first job and make their own money. These teens are on their way. They have new interests and desires for freedom. This opens up a new world of self-determination, choices, responsibilities, and consequences. They have a passion to be treated as an equal by their elders. As they travel from adolescents to early adulthood, they are declaring their independence.

Establish Independence

According to Wikipedia, Young adults are at a time when there are changes. There is a move to independence. Changes in relationships with parents, peers and others in society occur. The teenage mind and how its development affects rational and irrational decisions are obvious by the choices they make.

Many teens want a lot of freedom, but can only handle small doses. The young adult stage involves the need to socialize and make new friends. Failure to achieve this need can results in isolation. Young adults can become overwhelmed trying to make a living and taking on the responsibility of supporting a family. Many delay this responsibility to finish their education.

Most young adults work while continuing their education. For some young adults, this transition from childhood to becoming an adult can be traumatic. These can include fear, anxiety, depression, stress or feelings of loneliness and isolation. It is sometimes difficult to differentiate between normal adolescent emotions and serious mental health difficulties.

Among the mental health "red flags" you should be alert for are:

- Excessive sleeping, beyond usual teenage fatigue, which could indicate depression or substance abuse; difficulty in sleeping, insomnia, and other sleep disorders

- Abandonment or loss of interest in favorite pastimes

- Unexpected and dramatic decline in academic performance

- Weight loss and loss of appetite, which could indicate an eating disorder

- Personality shifts and changes, such as aggressiveness and excess anger that are sharply out of character and could indicate psychological, drug, or sexual problems

- Loss of self-esteem

Signs Low Self-Esteem

According to the American Academy of Pediatrics, the transition from childhood to becoming an adult can cause low self-esteem. Feelings of low self-worth and isolation can cause them to develop a negative self-image. To help you determine if your child has low self-esteem, watch for the following signals. They could be everyday responses to how your child relates to the world around him, or they might occur only occasionally in specific situations. When they become a repeated pattern of behavior, you need to become sensitive to the existence of a problem.

- He quits soon after beginning a game or a task, giving up at the first sign of frustration.

- He cheats or lies when he believes he's going to lose a game or do poorly.

- He shows signs of regression, acting baby-like or very silly. These types of behavior invite teasing and name-calling from other youngsters, thus adding insult to injury.

- He becomes controlling, bossy, or inflexible as ways of hiding feelings of inadequacy, frustration, or powerlessness.

- He makes excuses ("The teacher is dumb") or downplays the importance of events ("I don't really like that game anyway"), uses this kind of rationalizing to place blame on others or external forces.

- His grades in school have declined, or he has lost interest in usual activities.

- He withdraws socially, losing or having less contact with friends.

- He experiences changing moods, exhibiting sadness, crying, angry outbursts, frustration, or quietness.

- He makes self-critical comments, such as "I never do anything right," "Nobody likes me," "I'm ugly," "It's my fault," or "Everyone is smarter than I am."

- He has difficulty accepting either praise or criticism.

- He becomes overly concerned or sensitive about other people's opinions of him.

- He seems to be strongly affected by negative peer influence, adopting attitudes and behaviors like a disdain for school, cutting classes, acting disrespectfully, shoplifting, or experimenting with tobacco, alcohol, or drugs.

Parents should be attentive to adolescent behavior. Adolescence is a time of transition and change, but severe, dramatic, or abrupt changes in behavior can be strong indicators of serious mental health issues.

Developing Healthy Self-Esteem

Healthy self-esteem means thinking as highly of yourself as you think of your friends and peers. We are so used to negative feedback that we are more aware of our weaknesses than our strengths. We are often taught we will "fail", so it is often hard to enjoy success, no matter how small each "success" might be.

What is Self-Esteem? According to Nathaniel Branden, Ph.D., noted author and expert on the subject, "Self-esteem is the experience of being competent to cope with the basic challenges of life and of being worthy of happiness."

Why is High Self-Esteem Necessary? As Branden notes, "Positive self-esteem is the immune system of the spirit, helping an individual face life problems and bounce back from adversity." So, high self-esteem is crucial during the turbulence of your teenage years.

How Can A Teen Build Self-Esteem? The process is simple, but putting it to work is difficult. Self-esteem is built upon the experience of success. Think of it as a circular process. When people experience success, they grow in self-confidence. As self-confidence grows, they feel empowered to face new challenges. As they succeed in confronting each challenge, they develop the capacity to cope with whatever life throws their way. That feeling leads to further growth of self-confidence, self-reliance and self-esteem.

To Maintain Healthy Self-Esteem:

- Celebrate your strengths and achievements.

- Forgive yourself for your mistakes.

- Don't dwell on your weaknesses, every human has them.

- Change the way you talk to yourself. Stop putting yourself down!

- Be sure that you are not judging yourself against unreasonable standards.

- Beating yourself for your weaknesses is self defeating. Use that energy for positive thoughts about you.

High self-esteem means comparing your value to others' and finding yourself superior. It gives a sense of confidence. High self-esteem is seen as being the basis for career success and good relationships with other people. Source: www.coolnurse.com

CHAPTER 4

❖❖

The Challenges of Youth

Adolescent Love or Risky Behavior

How is love defined and what are the various types of love relationships? For each relationship type, essential skills are needed, and without these skills more advanced relationships are not possible. One of the major problems for adolescents during this period is learning how to channel sexual energy and drive into socially acceptable behaviors. It is difficult because the adolescent brain has not fully developed.

The human brain contains a huge number of chemical synapses. Young children have about 10 quadrillion synapses. This number declines with age, stabilizing by adulthood. Estimates for adults vary from 1-5 quadrillion synapses. The word "synapse" comes from "synaptein" coined from the Greek "syn-" ("together") and "haptein" ("to clasp"). As stated earlier research from the National Institutes of Health shows teen brains have extra synapses in the areas responsible for judging risks and making decisions. Many of these synapses are useless and get in the way of clear thinking.

During adolescence, three influences become important: sex, drugs, and motor vehicles. Teenagers can easily mistake sex for love, and having unprotected sex is risky business. Yes, they are trying to establishing their own identity and independent, but the impact is that if they're reckless, they must suffer the consequences. Teenagers have difficulties controlling their sexual impulses as they search for true love.

1st Corinthians 13:4-7 says, "Love is patient, love is kind. It does not envy, it does not boast, it is not proud. It is not rude, it is not self-seeking, it is not easily angered, and it keeps no record of wrongs. Love does not delight in evil but rejoices with the truth. It always protects, always trusts, always hopes, and always perseveres."

Types of Love

Wikipedia describes love as a basic dimension of human experience that manifests itself in feelings, emotion, behavior, thoughts, perception and attitude. Love is conveyed as a sense of tender affection, an intense attraction, the foundation of intimacy and good chemistry, willing self-sacrifice on behalf of another. Love is an important factor in intimate relationships. Research has established that love means more than merely liking a lot, and is distinct from sexual attraction. Passionate love is intense longing, and is often accompanied by physiological arousal (shortness of breath, rapid heart rate). Companionate love is affection and a feeling of intimacy and is not accompanied by physiological arousal by itself.

There are many distinct classifications of love including: agape love; platonic love; parental love; love at first sight; casual love.

Agapē Love: The word "*agapo*" is the verb "I love". This word represents divine, unconditional, self-sacrificing, active, volitional, thoughtful love. The term agape is used by Christians to refer to the special love for God and God's love for humanity, as well as the self-sacrificing love that all should have for each other. Greek philosophers use the term to denote love of a spouse or family. *Eros* (ἔρως *érōs*) is passionate love, with sensual desire and longing. E*ros*, is an affection of a sexual nature.

Parental Love is the unconditional love of a parent for their child; this type of love is a deep bond. Parental love is the first love a child experiences. Parental love should be nurturing, caring, stable, and attentive to children's needs. Parents are role models showing children love and how to love.

Platonic Love is an affectionate relationship into which the sexual element does not enter, according to Wikipedia. A simple example of platonic relationships is a deep, non-sexual friendship between two people. A deeply moving relationship that is based on Ephesians 4:2 **says,** "With all lowliness and meekness, with longsuffering, forbearing one another in love."

Love at First Sight is instant chemistry, when a person feels romantic passion for a complete stranger upon his or her initial encounter. It usually refers to actually falling in love with someone literally the very first time one sees him or her, along with the deep desire to have an intimate relationship with that person, usually when their eyes meet.

Types of Relationships

Infatuation: The typical adolescent infatuation may lead to marriage and a family, but intimacy of any sophistication is a matter between mature adults, settled men and women who realize that a well conducted liaison can enrich and refine the spirit like a work of art.

Dating/Courtship: Wikipedia says dating/courtship is the process of selecting and attracting another for an intimate relationship such as love, sex, commitment, living together, marriage, and having children, or any combination of these. Dating/courtship may last days, months, or even years.

Casual Relationships: Extends beyond *one night stands* that exclusively consist of sexual behavior. The participants may be known as *friends with benefits* when limited to considering sexual intercourse or sexual partners in a wider sense.

Love-Hate Relationship: The term comes from the way one may love the person one moment, and yet the next moment feel great rage or hatred for loving that person. There remains a high degree of sexual intimacy, but the emotional intimacy has degraded or vanished altogether. The relationship is held together by the hatred each person conjures. This anger is the cover up for the *"love"* part of the relationship because the couple dislikes social knowledge of the affair. The hate is also powered by the teasing of each person while the frustration reaches its maximum level through the restriction on releasing their sexual tension and intimacy. Blaise Pascal once said, "The heart has reasons which reason cannot understand."

Love Addiction: which is also a kind of love-hate relationship. Some in these circumstances have observed that the overall emotional feeling is not wholly unlike an actual substance-abuse addiction.

Risky forms of behavior can be caused by peer pressure. When a child feels like another kid was trying to get you to do something you didn't want to do; they feel peer pressure. The individual's values are tested by experiences outside the family.

Peer Pressure

The complications of interaction between parent and adolescent are compounded by the teens striving for independence, by the increasing important of his/her peer group, and by changing social influences. Because of rapid social change, many contemporary adolescent experiences fall outside of the range of parental understanding. Furthermore, many teens feel that his/her parents do not try to understand their problems. Both parents and adolescents bear responsibility for increasing their communications, although parents may have to initiate new activities and new forms of communications.

According to Dr. Gary Collins, peers are of significance as adolescents seek to break away from parental influences, values, and control. The family still provides money, transportation, and a place to live, but teenagers often criticize parental standards and have no desire to accompany parents to church, on vacations, or on shopping trips. Communication at home may be minimal, but daydreaming is common and long hours are spent talking with friends on the telephone. There is a great desire to be accepted and to identify with current teenage language, heroes, music, styles of dress, and forms of entertainment. Dating or other relationships with the opposite sex become of extreme significance and "breakups" are very painful.

Cars and motorcycles also lead to greater acceptance from peers and provide a way to express power or strengthen feelings of insecurity. As hormones rage, peer pressure may lead to premature sex.

The National Youth Anti-Drug Media Campaign says that sometimes, teens lack the language needed to help them stay away from risky situations. Here are some lines you can provide to your teen with in the event that he or she is offered drugs by his or her friends:

- "No, thanks. It's not for me."
- "Why would I want to mess up a good thing? I'm cool the way I am."
- "You're kidding, right? Why would I do something so dumb?"
- "No way, man. Taking drugs is stupid."
- "Can't do it. Gotta get home."
- "I tried drinking and got sick."
- "That's illegal. I don't want to get in trouble."
- "I have a big game tomorrow."
- "I'm up for a scholarship and don't want to blow it."
- "My parents would kill me."
- "My cousin smoked marijuana and got caught by the police."
- "I can't use drugs. I have a big test tomorrow."
- "I could get kicked off the team if anyone found out."

Risky Behavior

As stated previously, three influences become important to teenagers: sex, drugs, and motor vehicles. The need for love and acceptance, the influence of sexual hormones, and the sexual openness in our society, make sexual intercourse a common experience for adolescents.

Children at higher risk for involvement in violence and crime include boys born to teen mothers, children from families whose parents never completed high school and young people doing poorly in school. A young poor child is more likely than a non-poor one to be a current victim and a later perpetrator of violent crime. It takes more intense reward to stimulate a teen's brain and that could lead some to take risks ranging from extreme sports to drinking or drugs.

Brain maturation is still going on well into adulthood. A parent's responsibility is to help their teen transition into adulthood. This means giving your views and judgment to fall back on until they're ready to rely on their own.

In addition, young people use alcohol and other drugs at high rates. Adolescents are more likely to engage in high-risk behaviors, such as unprotected sex, when they are under the influence of drugs or alcohol. In 2005, 23% of high school students who had sexual intercourse during the past three months drank alcohol or used drugs before last sexual intercourse.

Abstinence from vaginal, anal, and oral intercourse is the only 100% effective way to prevent HIV, other STDs, and pregnancy. The correct and consistent use of a male latex condom can reduce the risk of STD transmission, including HIV infection. However, no protective method is 100% effective, and condom use cannot guarantee absolute protection against any STD or pregnancy.

Adolescent Sexuality

Sexual activity in humans is an instinctive form of physical intimacy. It may be performed for the purposes of biological reproduction, expressing affection, and/or for pleasure and enjoyment (known in this context as "sexual gratification"). The desire to have sex is one of the basic drives of human behavior.

Every sexually reproductive animal species, and every human culture, has a range of conduct used in courtship, intimacy, and sexual activity.

According to Wikipedia, human sexual behavior is the behaviors that human beings use when seeking sexual or relational partners, gaining approval of possible partners, forming relationships, showing affection, and mating. It covers at least two major areas: anthropology (common or accepted practices across different cultures), and informational (background which is useful to individuals who may be engaged in, or considering, sexual activity). Choosing chastity is an option even though hormones are raging during puberty.

Chastity

Chastity is often taken to be synonymous with virginity or abstention from all sexual activity. In many religious and cultural contexts, is a virtue concerning the state of purity of the mind and body, says Wikipedia. The term is most often associated with refraining from sexual intimacy, especially outside of marriage.

Cognitively Ready

Research has shown that cognitive control over high-risk behaviors is still maturing during adolescence, making teens more apt to engage in risky behaviors. The Oxford dictionary defines cognitive as the process of obtaining knowledge through thought, experience, and the senses. According to Dr. Liz Alderman, an adolescent medicine specialist at Montefiore Medical Center, adolescents in the United States are now physically ready for sex before they are emotionally or cognitively ready. Many teens have a sexual life, whether they're active sexually or through fantasies. Many other teens have chosen abstinence. Studies have found that the average age girls are entering puberty has remained steady since the 1960s.

Some adolescents are prone to desire and ready to carry out any desire they have fashioned into action. They apply no self-restraint, particularly when it comes to sex. When it comes to sex, teens must ask themselves some very important questions? These are questions no one else can answer. However, they should remember that having sex has consequences, and that include the potential for pregnancy and STDs.

- There is no correct age at which you are "supposed" to have sex. Everyone has to make a very personal decision about what is right for them. How does one decide when the time is right to have sex for the first time? Asking the following questions is a good start and might help decide how one really feels without the pressure from friends or that "special person": Does he/she want to wait until they are married because they have moral or religious convictions that might make deciding to have sex the wrong decision for them?

- What does he/she think might happen as a result of having sex? Do they really understand the potential consequences? Do they understand physical and emotional consequences?

- Does he/she feel pressured to have sex? Is there pressure from their partner, friends or any other reason?

Sexually Transmitted Diseases

National Center for Chronic Disease Prevention and Health Promotion states that vaginal, anal, and oral intercourse place young people at risk for HIV infection and other sexually transmitted diseases (STDs). Vaginal intercourse carries the additional risk of pregnancy. In the United States

- In 2005, 47% of high school students had ever had sexual intercourse, and 14% of high school students had had four or more sex partners during their life.

- In 2005, 34% of currently sexually active high school students did not use a condom during last sexual intercourse.

- In 2002, 11% of males and females aged 15-19 had engaged in anal sex with someone of the opposite sex; 3% of males aged 15-19 had had anal sex with a male.

- In 2004, an estimated 4,883 young people aged 13-24 in the 33 states reporting to CDC were diagnosed with HIV/AIDS, representing about 13% of the persons diagnosed that year.

- Each year, there are approximately 19 million new STD infections, and almost half of them are among youth aged 15 to 24.

- In 2000, 13% of all pregnancies, or 831,000, occurred among adolescents aged 15-19.

More Risky Behavior

According to CDC's Youth Risk Behavioral Survey (YRBS), many young people begin having sexual intercourse at early ages: 47% of high school students have had sexual intercourse, and 7.4% of them reported first sexual intercourse before age 13. Many adolescents are prone to desire and ready to carry out any desire they have formed into action. They exercise no self-restraint, especially when it comes to sex.

HIV/AIDS education needs to take place at correspondingly young ages, before young people engage in sexual behaviors that put them at risk for HIV infection.

Almost all US teens reported having used at least one form of contraception during intercourse, but only 75% of females aged 15-19 used some method of contraception the first time they had sex. In addition, 46% report not having used a condom the last time they had sexual intercourse. Every year 1 in 4 sexually active teens contracts an STD. The number of Adolescents having sexual intercourse has dropped in recent years, but oral sex is on the rise. Given their incomplete emotional and cognitive development (changes in mental process), adolescents are also particularly at risk to suffer from emotional distress as a result of their sexual activities.

Risky behavior can lead to AIDS: Statistics in 2004 shows that HIV/AIDS data from the 35 areas with long-term, confidential name-based HIV reporting.

- An estimated 4,883 young people received a diagnosis of HIV infection or AIDS, representing about 13% of the persons given a diagnosis during that year.

- HIV infection progressed to AIDS more slowly among young people than among all persons with a diagnosis of HIV infection.

- The following are the proportions of persons in whom HIV infection did not progress to AIDS within 12 months after diagnosis of HIV infection:
    o   81% of persons aged 15–24
    o   70% of persons aged 13–14
    o   61% of all persons

- African Americans were disproportionately affected by HIV infection; accounting for 55% of all HIV infections reported among persons aged 13–24.

- During 2001–2004, in the 33 states with long-term, confidential name-based HIV reporting, 62% of the 17,824 persons 13–24 years of age given a diagnoses of HIV/AIDS were males, and 38% were females.

Teen Pregnancy

In the United States teenage pregnancy is a factor affecting a fourth of all U.S. teens under 18 years of age, who had been pregnant at least once (Alan Guttmacher Institute 1994). The National Center for Health Statistics (1999) shows that nearly 13% of all U.S. births in 1997 were to teenagers ages 15 to 19. Half of pregnant teenage mothers have an abortion and 3% give it up for adoption. (Tiezi, Lorain: Kulman, Linda)

Most teenagers don't plan to get pregnant, but many do. Teen pregnancies carry extra health risks to the mother and the baby. They require special understanding because depression is also common among pregnant teens. They need medical care, and education--particularly about nutrition, infections, substance abuse, and complications of pregnancy. In many cases, teenagers don't receive timely prenatal care. Teens also have a higher risk for pregnancy-related high blood pressure and its complications, and risks for the baby include premature birth and a low birth weight. During pregnancy, expecting mothers should avoid smoking, alcohol and drugs, all of which can damage the developing fetus, along with poor eating habits.

The teenage mother has special problems, physically and emotionally.

*The death rate from pregnancy complications is much higher among girls who give birth under age 15 than among older mothers.

*The teenage mother is more likely to be undernourished and suffer premature or prolonged labor.

*During the first three months of pregnancy; seven out of ten pregnant teenagers do not see a doctor or go to a clinic.

Compared to peers who delay childbearing until age twenty or later, young mothers are the most at-risk for being unfit parents because they are uncertain about their roles and may be frustrated by the continuous demands of caretaking; young mothers are more probable to be poor, to be a victim of physical violence, to have another child before reaching adulthood. She is more likely to drop out of school, to have unsteady employment, to be on public assistance, and to be less skilled.

Babies born to teenagers are at risk for neglect and abuse because their young mothers are uncertain about their roles and may be frustrated by the constant demands of caretaking.

Being a Teen Parent is a Reality

Here is what four young mothers stated:

• *"I got pregnant a month before my 17th birthday. My son's father and I got married five months ago and we're already separated. I live in an emergency shelter for teen moms. I raise my son alone. My son will be a year old next week. In his whole life, his father has only taken care of him by himself one time. He does not pay me child support...I have only been out once without him. The rest of the time he goes everywhere with me. I only get four hours of sleep at night. I have no money because I quit work to go back to school, and I'm not on public aid at the moment. I miss my friends. I don't see them anymore because they have their own lives. All I do is sit at home...I love my son more than anything in the world, but it would have been a lot better if this had happened when I was like 27 instead of 17."*

- *"What troubles me is when another girl finds out that I have a daughter and she says "that is so neat." A car is neat, an outfit is neat, and a baby is not. They take a lot of time and work. When you become a mom, you become responsible (physically, emotionally, and financially) for a child for the rest of your life. There are no weekends or summer vacations; the child will always be there. And no matter how good your relationship was before you became pregnant, the father will most likely have gone on his merry way. If I had been better informed, I would have never had sex in the first place, let alone a child."*

- *"Teen girls are faced with so many challenges in everyday life. We have so many decisions and choices to make will affect the rest of our lives like smoking, drinking, boys, grades, parents, friends, peer pressure...just to name a few. I think that these problems relate to teen pregnancy because all a teenage girl wants to do is to fit in and be accepted by her peers. Unfortunately, I think that some girls are so stuck on this idea of belonging that they will go any distance to fulfill it - including having sex. I hope that girls would look for another way to get involved instead of becoming pregnant."*

- *"Some girls today don't have stable lives. Also, girls today have low self-esteem and guys know this and take advantage of these girls, saying things like 'I love you. If you love me, blah blah blah...' These girls think that someone finally likes them and give in. Then they come out pregnant and ruin their lives because the guy doesn't stick around."*

Having more youth development programs that improve youth's education, career planning, and work opportunities will possibly decrease teen chances of risky behavior, such as unprotected sex and pregnancy. These programs are intended to develop life-skills without focusing on reproductive health issues. Research conducted in the U.S. and internationally shows support of youth development programs. Trends in this country imply the potential success of this type of approach: during the decades of the 50's, 60's and 70's, women were postponing marriage and childbirth for the sake of pursuing education and careers, teen pregnancy rates fell dramatically. There have been many positive evaluations of existing programs.

By preventing children from having children, we can address many difficult social problems, such as poverty that comes from generations of teen childbearing.

Ten Things Teens Want Parents to Know About Teen Pregnancy

You may be surprised to learn that young people do want to hear from parents and other adults about sex, love, and relationships. They say they appreciate - even crave - advice, direction, and support from adults who care about them. But sometimes, they suggest, adults need to change *how* they offer their guidance. Simply put, they want real communication, not lectures and not threats.

1. **Show us why teen pregnancy is such a bad idea.**
For instance, let us hear directly from teen mothers and fathers about how hard it has been for them. Even though most of us don't want to get pregnant, sometimes we need real-life examples to help motivate us.

2. **Talk to us honestly about love, sex, and relationships.** Just because we're young doesn't mean that we can't fall in love or be deeply interested in sex. These feelings are very real and powerful to us. Help us to handle the feelings in a safe way - without getting hurt or hurting others.

3. **Telling us not to have sex is not enough.** Explain why you feel that way, and ask us what we think. Tell us how you felt as a teen. Listen to us and take our opinions seriously. And no lectures, please.

4. **Whether we're having sex or not, we need to be prepared.** We need to know how to avoid pregnancy and sexually transmitted diseases.

5. **If we ask you about sex or birth control, don't assume we are already having sex.** We may just be curious, or we may just want to talk with someone we trust. And don't think giving us information about sex and birth control will encourage us to have sex.

6. **Pay attention to us before we get into trouble.** Programs for teen moms and teen fathers are great, but we all need encouragement, attention, and support. Reward us for doing the right thing - even when it seems like no big thing. Don't shower us with attention only when there is a baby involved.

7. **Sometimes, all it takes not to have sex is not to have the opportunity.** If you can't be home with us after school, make sure we have something to do that

we really like, where there are other kids and some adults who are comfortable with kids our age. Often we have sex because there's not much else to do. Don't leave us alone so much.

8. **We really care what you think, even if we don't always act like it.** When we don't end up doing exactly what you tell us to, don't think that you've failed to reach us.

9. **Show us what good, responsible relationships look like.** We're as influenced by what you do as by what you say. If you demonstrate sharing, communication, and responsibility in your own relationships, we will be more likely to follow your example.

10. **We hate "The Talk" as much as you do.** Instead, start talking with us about sex and responsibility when we're young, and keep the conversation going as we grow older.

What Teens Want Other Teens to Know About Preventing Teen Pregnancy

1. Thinking "it won't happen to me" is stupid; if you don't protect yourself, it probably will. Sex is serious. Make a plan.

2. Just because you think "everyone is doing it," doesn't mean they are. Some are, some aren't and some are just lying.

3. There are a lot of good reasons to say "no, not yet." Protecting your feelings is one of them.

4. You're in charge of your own life. Don't let anyone pressure you into having sex.

5. You can always say "no" even if you've said "yes" before.

6. If you think birth control "ruins the mood," consider what a pregnancy test will do to it.

7. If you're drunk or high, you can't make good decisions about sex. Don't do something you might not remember or might really regret.

8. Sex won't make him yours, and a baby won't make him stay.

9. Not ready to be someone's father? It's simple: Use protection every time or don't have sex.

The Public Costs of Teen Childbearing

Teen childbearing in the United States costs taxpayers (federal, state, and local) at least **$9.1 billion**, according to a 2006 report by Saul Hoffman, Ph.D. and published by the National Campaign to Prevent Teen Pregnancy. Most of the costs of teen childbearing are associated with negative consequences for the children of teen mothers, including increased costs for health care, foster care, and incarceration.

According to the National Campaign to Prevent Teen and Unplanned Pregnancy, only 40 percent of young teen mothers graduate from high school, compared to about three quarters of women who delayed their first birth to age 20-21 (Hoffman). Another 23 percent of young teen mothers earn a GED. Even so, when high school completion and a GED are combined, there is still a very large gap (more than 20 percentage points) in completion rates...Moreover, economic research suggests that a GED degree is not equivalent to a high school degree in terms of its labor market value (Cameron and Heckman).

Much less is known about the fathers of children born to adolescent mothers and about how a mother's age at first birth affects the earnings prospects of her child's father. A 1996 study found that over the first 18 years following the birth of their first child, the fathers of children born to mothers age 17 and younger earn, on average, $27,000 less than the fathers of children born to mothers age 20-21 (Brien and Willis). This amount is the net of the impact of other risk factors associated with being the partner of a young mother, factors that further tend to reduce labor market earnings. Based on the Brien and Willis study, Maynard in *Kids Having Kids* estimated that early births cost the public sector $1.7 billion in 1996 in the form of the lower taxes paid by these fathers on their lower earnings.

No new study of the impact of early births on fathers is available. It is, however, possible to construct a 2004 estimate by adjusting the 1996 estimate for changes in the price level between 1996 and 2004, the number of teen births, and the probability that a birth will be non-marital. Doing so suggests that teen births reduced the taxes paid by the fathers of the children of young teen mothers by a total of $1.7 billion annually over the first fifteen years after a birth.

The progress the nation made in reducing teen childbearing between 1991 and 2004 has already had a very substantial effect on public sector costs. This is due in large part to the dramatic decrease in the birth rate to teens aged 15-17 and the particularly large public sector costs of births to this age group (most of which, as noted earlier, attach to the children of these young teen mothers). It is not known exactly how much higher the costs of teen births in 2004 would have been had the teen birth rates not fallen, because it is not known exactly which women would have had births and whether a teen birth would have affected their lives and the lives of their children in exactly the same way that a birth affected the lives of the women who did have a birth in 2004. Still a reasonable assumption can be made. On average, if the costs imposed by those additional births were comparable to the costs of the teen births that actually occurred in 2004, then the annual total costs of all teen births would have been $15.8 billion, rather than $9.1 billion. In other words, the decline in the teen birth rates between 1991 and 2004 saved $6.7 billion in 2004 alone.

YOUTH RISK BEHAVIOR SURVEY

Percentage of students who seriously considered attempting suicide during the past 12 months Year 2005 United States

Grade	Sex	
T	T	16.9 (±0.9)
	F	21.8 (±1.3)
	M	12.0 (±1.0)
9	T	17.9 (±2.1)
	F	23.9 (±2.6)
	M	12.2 (±2.7)
10	T	17.3 (±1.6)
	F	23.0 (±2.0)
	M	11.9 (±2.0)
11	T	16.8 (±1.8)
	F	21.6 (±3.0)
	M	11.9 (±1.9)
12	T	14.8 (±1.7)
	F	18.0 (±2.7)
	M	11.6 (±2.1)

Sex T=Total F=Female M=Male
Grade T=Total 9=9th Grade 10=10th Grade 11=11th Grade 12=12th Grade

Youth Suicide

The overall rate of suicide among youth has declined slowly since 1992 (Lubell, Swahn, Crosby, and Kegler 2004). However, rates remain unacceptably high. Adolescents and young adults often experience stress, confusion, and depression from situations occurring in their families, schools, and communities. Such feelings can overwhelm young people and lead them to consider suicide as a "solution." Few schools and communities have suicide prevention plans that include screening, referral, and crisis intervention programs for youth.

- Suicide is the third leading cause of death among young people ages 15 to 24. In 2001, 3,971 suicides were reported in this group (Anderson and Smith 2003).

- Of the total number of suicides among ages 15 to 24 in 2001, 86% (n=3,409) were male and 14% (n=562) were female (Anderson and Smith 2003

For all young people between ages 10 to 24, the suicide rate rose 8 percent from 2003 to 2004 — the biggest single-year bump in 15 years — in what one official called "a dramatic and huge increase."

The report, based on the latest numbers available, was released in September 2007 by the Centers for Disease Control and Prevention and suggests a troubling reversal in recent trends. Suicide rates had fallen by 28.5 percent since 1990 among young people.

The biggest increase was in the suicide rate for 10- to 14-year-old girls. There were 94 suicides in that age group in 2004 compared to 56 in 2003, a 67 percent increase. The rate is still low — fewer than one per 100,000 population.

Suicide rates among older teen girls, those aged 15-19 shot up 32 percent; rates for males in that age group rose 9 percent.

Overall, there were 4,599 suicides among young people in 2004, making it the third-leading cause of death, surpassed only by car crashes and homicide, Arias said. Males committed suicide far more often than females, accounting for about three-quarters of suicides in this age group.

The study also documented a change in suicide method. In 1990, guns accounted for more than half of all suicides among young females. By 2004, though, death by hanging and suffocation became the most common suicide method. It accounted for about 71 percent of all suicides in girls aged 10-14; about half of those aged 15-19; and 34 percent between ages 20-24.

Many teens, unable to cope with family situations such as parents divorcing, having to live with step-parents and step-siblings, school, and low self-esteem are stressed, confused, and depressed. Many see suicide as the only way out.

According to the American Academy of Child & Adolescent Psychiatry, depression and suicidal feelings are treatable mental disorders. The child or adolescent needs to have his or her illness recognized and diagnosed, and appropriate treatment plans developed. When parents are in doubt whether their child has a serious problem, a psychiatric examination can be very helpful. Many of the symptoms of suicidal feelings are similar to those of depression.

Parents should be aware of the following signs of adolescents who may try to kill themselves:

- change in eating and sleeping habits

- withdrawal from friends, family, and regular activities

- violent actions, rebellious behavior, or running away

- drug and alcohol use

- unusual neglect of personal appearance

- marked personality change

- persistent boredom, difficulty concentrating, or a decline in the quality of schoolwork

- frequent complaints about physical symptoms, often related to emotions, such as stomachaches, headaches, fatigue, etc.

- loss of interest in pleasurable activities

- not tolerating praise or rewards

A teenager who is planning to commit suicide may also:

- complain of being a bad person or feeling rotten inside

- give verbal hints with statements such as: I won't be a problem for you much longer, Nothing matters, It's no use, and I won't see you again

- put his or her affairs in order, for example, give away favorite possessions, clean his or her room, throw away important belongings, etc.

- become suddenly cheerful after a period of depression

If a child or adolescent says, I want to kill myself, or I'm going to commit suicide, always take the statement seriously and immediately seek assistance from a qualified mental health professional. People often feel uncomfortable talking about death. However, asking the child or adolescent whether he or she is depressed or thinking about suicide can be helpful. Rather than putting thoughts in the child's head, such a question will provide assurance that somebody cares and will give the young person the chance to talk about problems.

If one or more of these signs occurs, parents need to talk to their child about their concerns and seek professional help when the concerns persist. With support from family and professional treatment, children and teenagers who are suicidal can heal and return to a healthier path of development.

If children only knew that life changes daily, and that tomorrow is a new day and a new beginning. Don't turn on yourself, turn to loved ones or call hotlines. In any case, talk it out with someone. Thoughts and feelings change. Keep living. Teens should remember that no storm last forever.

Excerpts from *Your Adolescent* on Teen Suicide

That a teenager could be so unbearably unhappy that he would choose to kill himself is something that's almost too painful for a parent to examine. But with the increasing prevalence of teen suicide, no parent can afford to ignore the possibility.

Before the mid-1970s, suicide by adolescents appeared to be a rare event; now one out of ten teens contemplates suicide, and nearly a half million teens make a suicide attempt each year. Sadly, suicide has become the third leading cause of death for high-school students. Indeed, the actual rate of death by suicide may be higher, because some of these deaths have been incorrectly labeled "accidents."

Organizations that help teens

Covenant House

Hotline: Crisis line: 1-800-999-9999
Web: **http://www.covenanthouse.org/**
Provides crisis counseling for teens and their caregivers, as well as emergency shelter for runaway teens throughout the US.

Love is Respect, National Teen Dating Abuse Helpline

Phone: 1-866-331-9474
Phone: TTY: 1-866-331-8453
Web: **http://www.loveisrespect.org**
"loveisrespect, National Teen Dating Abuse Helpline is a national resource that can be accessed by phone or the internet. The Helpline and loveisrespect.org offer real-time one-on-one support from trained Peer Advocates. The National Domestic Violence Hotline operates loveisrespect, National Teen Dating Abuse Helpline from their call center in Austin, TX."

Drug and Alcohol Treatment Referrals

(800) DRUG-HELP

http://www.DRUGHELP.org

Provides advice and referrals to individuals about drug and alcohol treatment services, including local referrals to programs in the caller's area. Run by the federal Substance Abuse and Mental Health Services Administration. Operates 24 hours daily.

Girls and Boys Town National Hotline

formerly Boys Town National Hotline

(800) 448-3000

(800) 448-1833

http://www.boystown.org/hotline/crisis.htm

Kids and parents may call this hotline and speak directly to a counselor about issues related to substance abuse, violence, depression, or any other family problems. Counselors can make local referrals for services. Spanish-speaking counselors available. Operates 24 hours daily.

CHAPTER 5

When Love Turns Bad

A lot of teens are in abusive relationships. An abusive relationship is a relationship characterized by the use or threat of physical or psychological abuse. Abusive relationships are often characterized by jealousy, emotional withholding, infidelity, sexual coercion, verbal abuse, broken promises, physical violence, control games and power plays.

http://www.recovery-man.com/abusive/abusive.htm The rational part of a teenagers mind is not fully developed yet, which explains why teens think and act the way they do. Many teenagers are in violent relationships where mental and physical abuse takes place. Today, some people are literally, "loving their partners to death". If one partner tries to break-up or leave the relationship, murder-suicide occurs. An anonymous writer once wrote, "It is far better to forgive and forget than to resent and remember."

Teens at Risk in Abusive Relationships

Everyone has heard songs about how much love can hurt but that doesn't mean physical harm: Someone who loves you should **never** abuse you. Healthy relationships involve respect, trust, and consideration for the other person.

Teens must realize that they have the right to be treated with respect and not be physically or emotionally harmed by anyone.

People who abuse do so as a way to assert entire control over someone because they are weak and lack self-worth themselves. They want their partner to feel as bad as they do. It is a way to assert an identity and to use their partner as an object and tool for gratification. Often times, they have experienced abuse themselves, and they may not know another way to communicate. Regardless, an abusers background doesn't justify continuing abuse.

Abusive relationships are often progressive. That is, the abuse may get worse over time. Abusive relationships have become more commonplace in the home and elsewhere, and age, race and gender aren't factors. *Teenagers who become involved in abusive relationships are especially in danger because they lack the mental and emotional maturity to put an end to it.* The brain's reward center, the ventral striatum, also is more active during adolescence than in adulthood, and the adolescent brain still is strengthening connections between its reasoning- and emotion-related regions.

Abusive relationships can range from physical, emotional and sexual abuse. Each individual is responsible for their own actions, and each individual can seek help and change if they desire to. Adolescents and adults often don't make the link between dating abuse and poor health

Physical violence is usually accompanied by emotional or psychological abuse which can lead to various psychological consequences for victims such as:

- Depression
- Antisocial behavior
- Suicidal behavior
- Anxiety
- Low self-esteem
- Inability to trust people
- Fear of intimacy
- Social

Teens may remain in an abusive relationship for many reasons, including:

- Fear of the perpetrator
- Self-blame
- Minimization of the crime
- Loyalty or love for the perpetrator
- Social stigma or peer pressure

Adolescents in Abusive Relationship Are at Risk for Health Problems

- 70% of girls and 52% of boys who are abused report an injury from an abusive relationship. (Foshee 1996).

- 8% of boys and 9% of girls have been to an emergency room for an injury received from a dating partner (Foshee 1996).

- Victims of dating abuse are not only at increased risk for injury, they are also more likely to engage in binge drinking, suicide attempts, physical fights, and currently sexual activity (CDC 2006).

- Rates of drug, alcohol, and tobacco use are more than twice as high in girls who report physical or sexual dating abuse than in girls who report no abuse (Plichta 1996).

- Dating abuse is associated with unhealthy sexual behaviors that can lead to unintended pregnancy, sexually-transmitted diseases, and HIV infections (Silverman et al. 2001).

- Adolescents in abusive relationships often carry these unhealthy patterns of abuse into future relationships (Smith et al. 2003).

How Teens Can Recognize Abusive Relationships

Examples of Abuse

Abuse can be physical, sexual or emotional, which is the hardest to recognize. Slapping, hitting, and kicking are forms of physical abuse that can occur in both romances and friendships.

Emotional abuse, like teasing, bullying, and humiliating others, can be difficult to recognize because it doesn't leave any visible scars. Threats, intimidation, putdowns, and betrayal are all harmful forms of emotional abuse that can really hurt — not just during the time it's happening, but long after too.

It's never right to be forced into any type of sexual experience that you don't want. This type of abuse can happen to anyone, anytime.

How do you know if a Friend Is Being Abused? Abuse can sometimes be mistaken for intense feelings of caring or concern. Sometimes abuse can even seem flattering; think of a friend whose boyfriend or girlfriend is insanely jealous. Maybe you've thought your friend's partner really cares about him or her. But actually, excessive jealousy and controlling behavior are not signs of affection at all. Love involves respect and trust; it doesn't mean constantly worrying about the possible end of the relationship.

Here are some signs of abuse to look for in a friend:

- unexplained bruises, broken bones, sprains, or marks
- excessive guilt or shame for no apparent reason
- secrecy or withdrawal from friends and family
- avoidance of school or social events with excuses that don't seem to make any sense

A person who is being abused needs someone to hear and believe him or her. Maybe your friend is afraid to tell a parent because that will bring pressure to make him or her end the relationship. People who are abused often feel like it's their fault — that they "asked for it" or that they don't deserve any better. But abuse is **never** deserved. You need to help your friend understand that it is not his or her fault. Your friend is not a bad person. The person who is being abusive is at fault and needs professional help.

A friend who is being abused needs your patience, love, and understanding. Your friend also needs your encouragement to get help **immediately** from an adult, such as a parent or guidance counselor. Most of all, your friend needs you to listen to him or her without judging. It takes a lot of courage to admit being abused; let your friend know that you're offering your full support. How prevalence is dating violence?

Dating Violence

What Is Dating Violence?

Dating abuse is defined as the physical, sexual, or psychological/emotional violence within a dating relationship. Each year, 1 in 11 adolescent's reports being a victim of physical dating abuse (CDC 2006).

Many teens really do not know how to handle themselves when then find themselves in an abusive relationship. Many of these cases can be prevented by helping adolescents develop skills for healthy relationships with others (Foshee et al. 2005).

Dating Abuse Statistics

Adolescents and adults are often unaware how regularly dating abuse occurs.

- 1 in 11 adolescent's reports being a victim of physical dating abuse (CDC 2006).

- 1 in 4 adolescent's reports verbal, physical, emotional, or sexual abuse each year (Foshee et al. 1996; Avery-Leaf et al. 1997).

- 1 in 5 adolescent's reports being a victim of emotional abuse (Halpern et al. 2001).

- 1 in 5 high school girls has been physically or sexually abused by a dating partner (Silverman et al. 2001).

- Dating abuse occurs more frequently among black students (13.9%) than among Hispanic (9.3%) or white (7.0%) students (CDC 2006).

- 72% of eighth and ninth graders reportedly "date" (Foshee et al. 1996); by the time they are in high school, 54% of students report dating abuse among their peers (Jafe et al. 1992).

How to Prevent Dating Abuse

Dating abuse can be prevented. Adolescence has been characterized as a "window of opportunity" - a time for adolescents to prepare for future relationships by learning healthy relationship skills such as negation, compromise, and conflict resolution (Wolfe and Wekerle 1997). That's why adults need to talk to adolescents now about the importance of choosing respect and developing healthy relationships.

- Several studies suggest that adolescents do not see the negative consequences of dating abuse and violence in their friends' lives (Hotaling and Sugarman 1986). 31% of adolescents report having at least one friend who is in a violent relationship (Arriaga and Foshee 2004).

- Acceptance of dating abuse among friends is one of the strongest links to future involvement in dating abuse (Bergman 1992; Arriaga and Foshee 2004).

- Adolescents often believe that unhealthy relationships are the norm. Many relationships seen on TV, in the movies, and in magazines are unrealistic or unhealthy examples of relationships.

- Qualities like respect, good communication and honesty are absolute requirements for a healthy relationship. Adolescents that do not have this part down before they begin to date may have trouble forming healthy, nonviolent relationships with others (Wekerle and Wolfe 1999; Feiring and Furman 2000).

How Victims of Abuse Can Help Themselves

What should you do if you are experiencing from any type of abuse? If you can't love someone without feeling afraid, it's time to get out of the relationship now. You should be treated with respect and you **can** get help.

A trusted adult can help you and make sure you're safe. If someone has physically attacked you, get medical attention and call the police. Assault is illegal, and so is rape — even if it's done by someone you are dating.

Never isolate yourself from your friends and family. You need support the most when you feel like you have no one to turn to. They can help you get out of that situation. Never be embarrassed about what's been going on. There are many people trained and willing to help such as doctors, teachers, coaches, and counselors.

Don't rely on yourself alone to get out of the situation; the people who love and care about you can help you. It's important to know that asking for help isn't a sign of weakness. It shows that you are stronger than you think. Learn everything you can, educate yourself about domestic violence by reading various information in books or on-line.

How to end abusive relationships

Leave! Get out of that relationship

The best way to end an abuse relationship is to *leave* the person who is abusing you and disappear from their life. The sooner **you** end the relationship, the less severe the breakup will be. You have to end the abusive relationship don't expect the abuser to the end the relationship, because they usually won't. End all contact. And if you're wondering when to end the relationship, as soon as you notice he or she treats you badly. L*eave*. Don't believe them when they say they're sorry or they will change. He/she will most likely never change, without counseling. They'll change temporarily when there's no one there to abuse until the next victim comes along. All you can be responsible for is your own happiness. Take control of your life; don't let someone else control you.

Chapter 6

Adolescents Developing Life Skills

There are four parts to adolescence. We have covered physical, psychological, social, and now will cover the spiritual aspects. Spiritual qualities are necessary to develop our character which is the essence of who we are. Life skills, such as how to get along with people, integrity, honesty, and moral values are so important for adolescents. These are the building blocks for maturity. In order for teens to achieve this, family must have clear rules and consequences, and monitor the young person's whereabouts. Love your children, but you have to be the parent. Set the rules – stick by them. You are their keeper. Be a parent and not a pushover. Let the adolescent know what the rules are and your expectations. Make sure they know the consequences of breaking the rules. Let your teen express how they feel about the rules – give your teen a voice. Compromise some and most certainly let them see you care. These boundaries are beneficial in assisting young people to grow up to be healthy, caring, and responsible individuals. Teens learn core values at home and in church. In the past, moral values were taught and instilled in families, and character education was taught in school. Today there is a decline in morality and values in our society. A culture devoid of adherence to biblical standards is rapidly growing as a result of not sticking to Bible principles.

The duty of children is to obey their parents. That obedience includes inward respect, as well as outward acts. The duty of parents is not to be impatient, cruel or severely strict; but to nurture their children and carefully guide them. Bring them up well; under appropriate and considerate correction. God wants parents to instruct their children in His Word; to tell them of His judgments as Deuteronomy 32:46 says, ye shall command your children to observe. This parental duty is often unobserved, but this does not excuse the children's disobedience. God alone can change the heart, yet he gives his blessing to the good teaching and examples set by parents. The Bible says in Colossians 3:21 "Fathers, provoke not your children to anger, lest they be discouraged." Don't aggravate your children by cruelly and inappropriately finding fault with them, yelling or being difficult to please. Lest they be discouraged; despair of being able to please you, and so become broken in spirit. Commend and encourage them when they do well. This is good advice to help remain influential over your children.

Teenagers do benefit from obeying God's word daily. When they fail to obey His word for example in Ephesians Chapter 8 to obey their parents they sometimes get into trouble. Here is an example of a teenager who failed to obey God's Word. (I'll call her Brittany to protect her identity). Brittany is a very beautiful, well dressed Christian teenager. She has her own room, cell phone, computer and a part-time job. She attended church regularly, studied and made good grades in school. She had a close relationship with her parents and lots of nice friends. Over the course of several months, Brittany changed. She stopped going to church, stopped hanging out with her true friends. Her grades dropped, she began being very rude and disrespecting to her parents. Brittany got into a fight with one of her new friends, her old friends stopped calling her, and someone stole her cell phone. Things really started going down hill. Brittany remembered God's promise to us; He said in Ephesians, chapter 6, verses 1 through 3: "Children, obey your parents in the Lord: for this is right. Honor thy father and mother; which is the first commandment with promise that it may be well with thee, and thou may live long on the earth." Brittany realized that things would continue to go well for her and she would also have a long life if she would obey

God and her parents. She looked at her life, realized she made mistakes and needed to make changes. Brittany apologized to her parents and asked for their forgiveness. Her parents were happy and even bought her a new cell phone. Now she is attending church regularly and has made up with her old friends.

Spiritual guidance is especially necessary for adolescence because it helps them make the right moral choices in life. It teaches them to have virtue, honor, respect and character.

Taking Responsibility

As a teen goes through adolescence there are many life skills that must be learned along the way. There are values to be instilled such as moral guidance and training. How can teens grow and develop at home if they are not available, uncooperative and open to suggestions? Many missed opportunities turn into regrets later in life. As teens turn into young adults, they realize their mistakes and sometimes foolish choices such as dropping out of school or running away from home, or not listening to their parents or resisting their guidance experience and knowledge they want to pass on to their children. It is easy to withdraw from your family even society and justify a lack of communication. Blaming or criticizing others often lead to becoming defensive, self-righteous, and judgmental of others.

When teens are high on drugs or alcohol, how can parents communicate with them? Trust and being open and honest with each other is very important. Teens may blame their parents, saying they can't talk to them, but when they are confronted with their behavior they may lie, be rude and offensive or run away (if they do run away and want to return, welcome them back home). You're not the first family to go through this.

Teens must be responsible for their behavior. Responsibility is a moral issue. Teens need understanding, trust and support; not blame. Teens that are responsible for breaking trust with others must accept the consequences of their actions and make amends; that is being responsible for their actions. They must be responsible not only for what they say and how it affects others, but also their reactions and behavior. Negative, rude behavior wins the support of no one. Acts of forgiveness opens the way for further forgiveness. Teens must focus their attention and energy on themselves and their family and make compromises. Learn to do things that are for the good of the family. A parent must disengage from a teen who is trying to manipulate them. Parents must take a firm stand and not allow their teen/teens to divide them to get their ways. Teens must not ignore their parents and refuse to answer questions by being evasive or give one syllable answers; that is not open communication.

Teens must not act like know it alls, or think they know more than everyone else, especially their parents. Television today has programs that are cynical of parents, and make fun of long standing traditions. These social changes are affecting teens and societal views. Many families that have adapted these cynical views are reaping what they have sown; less caring, less supportive, less educated children. Many families suffer from domestic abuse, control manipulation and lack of spiritual guidance. Many people believe there is a higher power, yet fall short of obeying that source.

Parents must realize that they are role models, and children will do as they see their parents doing, not as they say. Actions speak louder than words. If a teen sees their parents lying, stealing, being promiscuous they will feel like their parents are hypocrites when they see them doing the same thing they tell their teen not to do. Teens need constructive criticism, not destructive criticism in order to grow, overcome their mistakes and try again. Teens with manipulating parents are teaching their teens how to be manipulative. Our lifestyles affect the way we view life and how we will rear and discipline our children.

Taking Responsibility in Extended Families

Becoming a step parent is challenging; accepting step adolescence into a family can create confusion, mistrust, anger and a host of other issues that families must deal with successfully during a period of adjustment. If a teen is on drugs or alcohol, the process of adjustment becomes impossible without help. The teen may be angry at both parents and refuse to respect the family arrangement. They won't cooperate and this causes a lot of strain on the family to the breaking point and many families call it quits and go their separate ways.

Many families unite into a happy blended extended family after a challenging period of adjustment. Feelings, thoughts, and emotions must be handled and settled. Actions must be taken not avoided. Commitment must be made and honored. Each family member must respect and accept guidance from both parents. Both parents must unit as one and not allow the children or adolescent to divide them in order to have their way. When spouses disagree they should never back up their kids whenever there is a conflict. Parents must show unity; never disagree or argue in front of their children, but resolve their difference in private.

Everyone in the family must feel loved, respected and appreciated. A father must not allow the adolescent to run the house and make the rules which is the parents' responsibility. It is not the teen's responsibility to break or make the rules, but to accept parental guidance and follow the rules even if they don't fit with their agenda. Parents must not break promises to their children. Broken promises cause children to feel bad about their selves and are left feeling unloved, rejected or even abandoned.

Limits and boundaries must be clear and consistent. Teens need a support system to help them learn and maintain coping skills. The support structure help teens overcome negative emotions and help motivate and inspire adolescents to positive actions.

What Teens Must Learn

- How to develop good study habits
- How to give a speech/presentation
- How to recognize and choose good friends
- Building trust, who to trust
- How to survive
- Coping skills
- Responsibility
- How to drive
- How to communicate effectively with others
- How to behave in society, at home and in school
- Not rebellious when being corrected by adult in authority, but look, listen and learn
- Domestic skills
- How to obtain a job and keep it
- How to save money

Establishing Boundaries

Boundaries and Expectations / Family boundaries

Two main things that parents must stand their grounds on concerning boundaries are lying and disrespect. Parents must hold teens accountable when they catch them in a lie, letting them know that this is unacceptable behavior. Even though they may loose their temper and yell, they must know there will be consequences to their bad behavior. It is critical that parents never compromise on teens lying and being disrespectful because teens are in transition into adulthood and these are part of their core values. Teens must establish relationship boundaries with friends. Don't let your peers or friends talk you into doing things you shouldn't.

Teens need to learn boundaries and self control when it comes to drinking. Interestingly, research now shows that there is an additional reason for young people to avoid binge drinking besides that of obeying God and staying alive. Binge drinking impacts brain development, especially the younger the individual is. Scientists are finding that this is because the adolescent brain is undergoing a shift in the areas where decisions are processed.

Independent Living Skills

Teens need to know the crucial concepts necessary for safe and successful independent living. They can achieve confidence through exploring and practicing real life situations. Teens should realize that today's choices create the future. Teens should be able to identify careers of interest, and be able to make an informed career decision. As teens transition into adulthood, they need to know how to take the right steps towards being on their own responsibly. Such life skills include:

- learning about college entrance requirements

- creating a resume and interview for a job

- how to purchase and maintain a car, obtain insurance

- create and live within a budget

- how to find, furnish, and maintain their own apartment or house

Teaching teens about nutrition, grocery shopping, home management, financial matters, saving, banking & credit, and budgeting/spending plan will help them develop life-long skills. They should be taught the following workplace skills:

- Proper workplace attire
- Being on time, following directions, assuming responsibility) that affect job retention and advancement
- Working cooperatively with others as a member of a team
- Should know what the "chain of command" is and how it works
- The importance of supervision and accept supervision
- The ability to manage time in order to complete work place tasks
- Identify ways to advance on the job (e.g. employment training programs, higher education)

Adolescents will transition to independent living with a solid knowledge of basic life skills reducing their chances of risky behavior, and help them chart a course for excellence in their lives.

Drinking Impacts Brain Development

Alcohol can inhibit, or even rewire, neuron development not only in the developing areas of the brain, but also in areas already developed. However, the teenage brain seems to have the ability to rebound if the teen stops using alcohol while this brain development is continuing.

According to Mothers Against Drunk Drivers, While alcohol-related traffic fatalities involving youth ages 15 to 20 have declined over the years, fatalities among that age group are now increasing to more than 2,400 deaths in 2002. Underage drinking kills 6,000 people annually, due to traffic crashes, homicides, suicides and unintentional injuries.

Motor vehicle crashes are the leading cause of death for U.S. teens, accounting for 36% of all deaths in this age group. In 2004, 4,767 teens ages 16 to 19 died of injuries caused by motor vehicle crashes (CDC 2006). The risk of motor vehicle crashes is higher among 16- to 19-year-olds than other age groups. Per mile driven, teen drivers ages 16 to 19 are four times more likely than older drivers to crash (IIHS 2006).

Risks from Unsafe Driving Behaviors

Teens are more likely than older drivers to underestimate hazardous situations or dangerous situations or not be able to recognize hazardous situations (Jonah 1987). Teens are more likely than older drivers to speed and allow shorter headways (the distance from the front of one vehicle to the front of the next). The presence of male teenage passengers increases the likelihood of these risky driving behaviors among teen male drivers. (Simons-Morton 2005).

Driving Rules to Live By

Understand the risks of choosing to drive unsafely.

1. Seat Belts—Every Trip, Every Passenger, Every Time

2. No Alcohol—No Drugs—No Pills

3. No Speeding—Ever

4. Stay Alert—No Drowsy Driving—No Distractions

5. Stay Cool—No Reckless Driving

Officials were concerned about the differing minimum drinking age between states and the number of teenagers dying in car accidents that they changed the law. On July 17, 1984, **President Ronald Reagan** signed the national 21 minimum drinking age legislation into law to eliminate the deadly "blood borders" between states that had differing minimum drinking age laws.

Adolescence is a time for growth and development, and many teens fall in love and they think that person is "the one" because love feels so right Some teens choose to marry at an early age, but research shows that the under developed minds of some teens are not capable of handling problems relating to life skills such as marriage.

Age of Reason

Coming of age or age of reason is a young person's transition from adolescence to adulthood. The age at which this transition takes place varies in society. Commonly 18 is the age adolescents are generally no longer considered minors and are granted the full rights of an adult.

According to Jay Giedd, chief of brain imaging in the child-psychiatry branch of the National Institute of Mental Health in Bethesda, Maryland, and author of "Teenagers' brains are not broken; they're just still under construction." Giedd has stated that the point of intellectual maturity, the so called "age of reason", comes about the age of 25. In women, it is reached a year or two earlier.

By most physical measures, teenagers should be the world's best drivers. Their muscles are supple, their reflexes quick, their senses at a lifetime peak. Yet car crashes kill more of them than any other cause. Some researchers believe this is rooted in the adolescent brain. A National Institutes of Health study suggests that the region of the brain that inhibits risky behavior is not fully formed until age 25, a finding with implications for a host of policies, including the nation's driving laws.

Teens are very impressionable, many believe what they see and read in magazines. They fall in and out of love quickly, they think they will love will last forever, but they seldom do. No matter how good the relationship starts off, the fact remains that it usually won't last.

True love last because it grows stronger and stronger with time, commitments are made which can last a lifetime. If you are truly in love, that love will still be there waiting when you are ready and mature enough to handle with the problems and issues of marriage.

CHAPTER 7

Teenage Life

What Teens Experience

Teenage life consists of a multitude of emotional peaks and valleys. They'll argue with parents and stop speaking to them one day, and the next day they want to bond with their parents (without apologizing or wanting to discuss the problem). The teenage years are exciting, filled with exploration and adventure on one hand; on the other hand teens tend to become rebellious against parents, society, and more critical of the values and principles of adult culture or way of life.

Even love through the eyes of teenagers has taken a drastic turn over the years. Teens experience growing pains such as awkward behavior, anger, and playing the blame game. They become self centered, focusing on themselves, their needs, and desires.

Much of today's sexually charged music, movies, and teen magazines promote their ideas of an adult lifestyle. This influences causes some teens too make decisions and live a lifestyle they may not be fully equipped mentally or emotionally to handle; trying to grow up too fast.

In the past teens had no choice about how they would spend their time. They knew their place and decisions were made for them. They knew the family structure and lifestyle and there was no questioning authority or disrespect tolerated. The father was the head of the household, the mother ran the house, cooked meals, she made sure the children did their chores and received an education.

Many teens today are demanding money, and free leisure time away from home. They want total freedom over their lives. They want to blame others rather than taking responsibility for their own actions.

Teens especially don't want to be told what to do or how to do it and have a strong need to be independent, which includes making their own choices and decisions. Teen choices and parental responsibilities often clash, as teens say yes and parents say no not yet, causing anger, resentment, disappointment and uncertainty on both sides. Typically, however, adolescents think that accepting parental values will put them out of step with their peers. If peer values are adopted, parental conflict may arise.

Some teens are talking back to their parent's, some are verbally, emotional or physically abusive to their parents. Some teen are deliberately withholding communication from their parents, which is a form of control.

When questioned about their activities many teens become irritated, impatient, short-tempered and quick to give one word answers, as they dodge issues and their parents, leaving parent to figure out what really is going on.

Some teens steal from their parents, drink, have sex or do drugs in their parent's home. Some teens throw wild parties at home sometimes with their parents permission. Some have killed their parents because of anger or greed. This type of negative behavior is based on irrational thinking.

What Teens Think

Teens think they should be given a lot of freedom, independence, and not asked a lot of questions about what they are doing. This can create tension, rebellion and power struggles. Parents understand the many pressures of adolescence and what they think their teens can handle often differs. What parents are willing to give, or think it is wise to give, may cause teens to be upset, angry, rebellious and uncorruptive.

Many teens do struggle with their problems alone. They keep things to themselves instead of going to their parents. Sometimes the parents are the last to know until their teen is forced to admit the truth. Things have gotten totally out of control and the parents looking for answers almost seek solutions.

Sometimes teens experience depression, anxiety, unexplained changes in mood or behavior. Even more common are how adolescence react to adjustments. They might be irritable, a brat, temper outbursts, violence, stealing, lying, smoking, drinking, acting out, failing in school subjects, challenging authority, gang behavior, resisting parents, asserting their independence, and sexual experimentation.

Teens often feel intense social pressure to experiment sexually, to experiment with alcohol, smoking and drugs. Sometimes this is just a cover-up to bolster self-esteem, to belong, and feel accepted. Many teens feel self-contempt and worthlessness as they get involved in empty relations, using others or being used as sex objects. There is an epidemic of venereal disease, unwanted pregnancies. Sometimes teens become self destructive, spiraling down into addictions, which effects can be devastating. Excessive drinking, eating disorders, suicide attempts is a cry for help, often they indicate a real desire to die. Many teens lash out in anger which can also be devastating to other family members.

Self esteem problems occur sometime because teens are lacking in social skills. Every teen challenge is to learn how to cope effectively, and transition from adolescence into adulthood many adolescence choices can have lifelong results. Being aware of this creates pressure and anxiety for teens to make the right choices, teens making wise choices must be a top priority of parents to steer their teens in the right direction.

Not all teens act out or make life difficult for themselves and their families. Many teens approach their teenage years with fun, joy, happiness and feel this is the best time of their lives. They love their family and support each other. They cooperate, trust, and value their family and relationships. They openly share their success and defeats. They allow others to contribute to their emotionally, socially, intellectually and spiritually. They pray together and worship together. There is no generation gap. Each generation is valued and appreciated. No one feels neglected, unworthy or lonely. Love has no boundaries within and love is easily shared and hugs and kisses are common. If someone withdraws or is sad, others rally around for support. In this healthy environment teens thrive and choose healthy relations with friends and associates who share the same values, choices and responsibilities and commitments. Parents have consistently displayed love, gentle persuasion, guidance, spiritual support, respect, trust, giving, sharing open honest communication. Parents have set boundaries and limitations.

Teens are incapable of making adult rational decisions because their brain is not fully developed yet, which explains why teens think and act the way they do. Many parents and church leaders fail to realize the intense pressures and problems facing teenagers today, which includes hormonal changes, sexual urges and the pressures to turn on with drugs and sex.

Parents need to understand what it's like to be an adolescent in today's society. With our changing technological and informational society and declining values teens are exposed to so much more temptations than in previous generations. Teens are under a lot more pressure and also must face many choices that their parents have never faced. An example is the internet which is being used for good and evil.

Teens have to be cautious and make wise decisions, or risk becoming potential victims. The problem is that teens are trying to make adult decisions inside a child's mind, which explains why many teens feel rules and restrictions are unfair.

Teens are growing up listening both to parents and peers as they attempt to make independent decisions. Teens have a strong desire to be with their peers and some are resisting adult's rules; but at the same time, this is the time teens need adults the most to complete their transition into adulthood.

Adults can make decisions because the adult mind is fully developed and equipped to think rationally when faced with troubling problems. As stated earlier, the rational part of a teenager's brain is not fully developed.

What Teens Want

- To have it their way
- To be left alone to achieve independence
- To make their own decisions
- To choose their friends.
- Some teens want to drink.
- Teens want parents to see their point of view
- Teens want cell phones to text each other
- To be able to get on the internet
- To play video games, watch TV and listen to their style of music

20 Teenage Regrets

1. Losing my virginity at age 17
2. Becoming a single parent
3. Joining a gang
4. Having a juvenile record
5. Not taking the ACT High School Test

6. Breaking up my friend's relationship by dating her boyfriend
7. Running away from home
8. Not following my dreams my passions
9. Not earning a degree
10. Getting married at age 19
11. Not going to college after High School and not going to church
12. Having unprotected sex and catching a STD
13. Growing up too fast by hanging out until late at night and getting high
14. Moving out on my on at age 16
15. Having an abortion
16. Not attending Church often after I turned 18
17. Arguing with my mom constantly and not appreciating her
18. Believing in fairy tales and happy endings
19. Not bonding with my older sister while we were growing up
20. Getting a girl pregnant-I'm too young to be a parent

The first national survey of its kind finds that virtually all American teens play computer, console, or cell phone games and that the gaming experience is rich and varied, with a significant amount of social interaction and potential for civic engagement. The survey was conducted by the Pew Internet & American Life Project, an initiative of the Pew Research Center and was supported by the John D. and Catherine T. MacArthur Foundation. The primary findings in the survey of 1,102 youth ages 12-17 concluded that game playing is universal, with almost all teens playing games and at least half playing games on any given day. Game playing experiences are diverse, with the most popular games falling into the racing, puzzle, sports, action and adventure categories.

Game playing is also social, with most teens playing games with others at least some of the time and can incorporate many aspects of civic and political life. As stated earlier, game playing sometimes involves exposure to mature content, with almost a third of teens playing games that are listed as appropriate only for people older than they are.

What Parents Want

- Their teens to be safe
- Their teens to get a good education
- Their teens to make good choices
- Their teens to be successful
- To monitor their teens selections; TV, music, and video games.
- To monitor their teens choice of friends
- To instill values in their teens so they will stay out of trouble

How Adults Can Help

According to Dr. Delores Livingston, Pastor and Educator, "parents need to offer adult guidance and supervision, identify and correct problems and negative behavior in their adolescence and not concentrate on being their friend." This type of parenting has been associated with positive outcomes in children. One of the factors contributing to the delinquency of teens is insufficient monitoring by parents after school.

Three basic ways in which the family assert its influence:
- *Power assertion*. This category includes physical punishment, the depriving the child of material objects

or privileges, and the directly applying force, or the threat of any of these.

- *Love withdrawal.* This category includes techniques whereby the parent more or less openly withdraws love by ignoring the child, turning his back on the child, refusing to speak to him, explicitly stating that he dislikes or isolation him.

- *Guilt induction regarding parents.* This mode of influence appeals to the child's guilt potential by referring to the consequences of the way the child treats the parent while attempting to establish independence.

Parents acting this way can breed hostility in the child.

Adults can also help by making this point plain to their teens: Alcohol alters a person's ability to think clearly. Clear thinking is especially important when driving. Teens like to socialize and

Teens love to attend parties, to have a good time and socialize. Many teens drink and drive. They may not know they are intoxicated or have impaired judgment. Teens may feel they are a good driver and it will be ok to drive, it is not. It is dangerous and they are risking not only their lives but also those who they come in contact with. Teens should never get in a car with anyone who has been drinking.

To keep your teen safe from drinking and driving, one solution would be to install an Intoxalock ignition system in the teen's car. This breath alcohol ignition interlock device is designed to prevent an individual from operating a motor vehicle while under the influence of alcohol. The result will be peace of mind for the parent and safety for the teen.

Five Self-help books for parents and teens

Lonely, Sad and Angry: A Parent's Guide to Depression in Children and Adolescents: Although only recently recognized by the mental health community (1980), childhood depression is very real, widespread, and treatable. This thoughtful book by two clinical child psychologists offers sound information on many aspects of the illness and guidance for treatment. Ingersoll and Goldstein fully and lucidly discuss the characteristics of depression in children and adolescents, coexisting conditions, diagnosis and evaluation, causes, and treatment options. They give detailed counsel on the worrisome issues of suicide and hospitalization, and they furnish reassuring and concrete advice for life at home and help at school. The coverage is thorough, noting newer research, and evenhanded, weighing pros and cons of psychotherapeutic approaches and medications. The scientific information is balanced by supportive and practical advice on the numerous challenges depressed children present. Noting that parents must make informed, critical decisions, Ingersoll and Goldstein enable parents to more confidently and intelligently recognize depression in their children, obtain professional help, determine treatment, cope with the daily struggles as well as the serious consequences, and gain hope for a more enlightened future.

Parenting Teens With Love & Logic: Preparing Adolescents for Responsible Adulthood: A unique approach to dealing with the turmoil of adolescence that recognizes that teens learn best when they're allowed to make choices and learn from the consequences. The trick is in setting up choices so the consequences are constructive.   Love means giving your teen opportunities to be responsible and empowering them to make their own decisions. Logic means allowing them to live with the natural consequences of their mistakes and showing empathy for the pain they will experience.   FOSTER CLINE, M.D., is an internationally recognized physician and adult and child psychiatrist who has successfully parented four children. JIM FAY has 31 years of experience as an educator and school principal

The 7 Habits of Highly Effective Teens: The Ultimate Teenage Success Guide:
Being a teenager is both wonderful and challenging. In *The 7 Habits of Highly Effective Teens,* author Sean Covey applies the timeless principles of the 7 Habits to teens and the tough issues and life-changing decisions they face. In an entertaining style, Covey provides a step-by-step guide to help teens improve self-image, build friendships, resist peer pressure, achieve their goals, get along with their parents, and much more. In addition, this book is stuffed with cartoons, clever ideas, great quotes, and incredible stories about real teens from all over the world. *The 7 Habits of Highly Effective Teens* will engage teenagers unlike any other book.

The Teenage Guy's Survival Guide: Peer pressure, body odor and kissing are just a few of the challenges faced in the straight-talking The Teenage Guys Survival Guide. The author does not shy away from controversial topics....and a mix of typefaces and a cartoon character provides a humorous running commentary, keep the text lively.

Teen-Proofing : A Revolutionary Approach to Fostering Responsible Decision Making in Your Teenager: With his trademark user-friendly, humorous, and common-sense style, John Rosemond lays out a perfectly sound and logical case for recognizing the realities of the teen/parent relationship, forming the foundation, and parenting with the Long Rope Principle. In short, the author demonstrates how mom and dad can avoid the pitfalls of becoming dictatorial Control Freaks, skirt the potholes of turning into permissive Wimps, and enjoy the freedom and rewards of parenting in a controlled (but not controlling) and relaxed manner. Infusing young adults with a sense of personal responsibility, then showing them the results of good and bad choices, is a goal every parent can achieve

Communicating With Your Teen

Communicate early and as often as possible; talk, listen, talk. Communication is especially important during teen years. Communication once effective and accepted by teens is now being challenged or rejected. Teens are causing parents to alter the way they communicate to fit the growing needs of adolescents. Most teens are growing up and are determined to gain independence, yet still retain close ties to their family. Research has shown adolescent adjustment has been linked with a balance of positive and negative discussions with parents.

A lot of parents and teens usually don't see eye to eye nor think the same way. It seems that no mater what topic the parent want to discuss, their teen don't see it that way. These teens may believe it's just old fashion ways of doing things that is coming from their parents and that things should be done another way,

What parents can do is to create an atmosphere in which all family members are free to discuss whatever topics they need to talk about. Teens need an opportunity for open and honest self-expression without him or her feeling pressured into sharing. They need to know that you accept and value his or her point of view; this has been linked to positive personality development.

Keep in mind these points about communication from the Child Development Institute:

- Turn off the television, avoid talking on the phone, and don't read the newspaper if your teen wants to talk.

- Let your teen know that you are interested and that you will help when needed.

- Hold conversations in private. The best communication between you and your teen should occur when others are not around.

- If you are angry about a behavior or an incident, don't attempt to talk until you calm down because you cannot be objective until then. Confront your teen with the information that you know or have been told.

- Listen carefully and don't interrupt your teen when he or she is trying to tell his or her story.

- Don't embarrass your teen in front of others. This will lead to resentment, not good communication.

- Keep adult talking to a minimum ("I know what's best for you." 'Just do what I say and that will solve the problem"), because they are not helpful in getting communication open and keeping it open.

- Praising his or her efforts to communicate. This helps to keep communication open.

Sensitive issues that arise during adolescence, such as sexuality and drug or alcohol use, can be discussed with greater comfort and success. In fact, research has shown that adolescents who share more openly with their parents are less likely to abuse substances and have closer loving relationships.

Principles to Nurturing Your Teenager

In a loving relationship, it is all about giving of oneself. Cardinal Mercia said, "We must not only give what we have; we must also give what we are." Teens can't help who they are; they can't yet function like an adult's. With the advent of technologies such as magnetic resonance imaging, neuroscientists have discovered that the adolescent brain is far from mature.

The 10 guiding principles below are from "Nurturing Your Teenager's Soul", A Practical Guide to Raising a Kind, Honorable, Compassionate Teen by Mimi Doe. This guide helps teens to develop an internal framework and moral compass to stay centered during turbulent years.

Principle 1: Realize You Are Part of Something Bigger

A connection with spirituality sustains teenagers throughout their inherently rocky transition into adulthood. A spirited life is much more than just decisions about faith. Kids want and need to define their own sense of spirituality. Parents can join their teens in this exploration process, as their children quest for an understanding of the universe and an individual sense of spirituality.

Principle 2: Understand that all Life is Connected and has Meaning

Adolescents need opportunities to recognize that they are not alone no matter how different from their peers they may feel. Teens hunger to be a part of something. Their need for acceptance runs deep. Support your teens in developing a deeper connection with the natural world, as nature unconditionally accepts them. Plus, social activism and reaching out to others in need gives teens the same assurance that they are connected and can make a difference.

Principle 3: Words Can Profoundly Change Lives

Tell your teenagers how they delight you, how much you respect their choices, your amazement at their abilities, or your appreciation of the way they solved a problem. We need to remember that teens typically struggle with a low self-image, at the same time that their need for love and acceptance is at an all time high. Now is the time to flood them with positive words. Loving words from a parent fuels a child, no matter their age.

Principle 4: Listen Fully and Acknowledge Deeply

In a 2004 survey by Spiritualparenting.com, teens were asked: "What do you wish your parents did differently?" The overwhelming response was unexpected. They didn't want more freedom, a later curfew, or another gadget. Instead, teens wished their parents actually listened to them more often.

Principle 5: Supported Dreams Manifest Miracles

By helping teens nurture their internal vision of who they are, we may be able to spare them years spent pursuing goals far astray from their personal dreams. We can help them find an authentic sense of purpose in the world: something that comes from connecting the deep currents in their hearts with the abilities of their hands and minds. When parents help kids identify what brings meaning to their daily activities, it's the answer to the fundamental spiritual question: "Why am I here?"

Principle 6: Awaken Wonder and Spirit Flows

Teens crave magic: that moment when time stands still and we're drawn outside our usual busy selves to find something rich and peaceful. Experiences and perceptions that go beyond the ordinary soothe a soulful yearning. But in the teen years, wide-eyed wonder isn't 'cool.' Teens have to learn how to silence their ever present internal critic in order to experience being fully present in an experience. It's hard to be in awe if you're worried about how your hair looks.

Principle 7: Remain Flexibly Firm

Parents have to be willing to shift the rules and become more flexible so their kids can mature into their fully-realized selves. By the time children reach their teen years, parents have gotten complacent about setting rules and creating family guidelines. The revisiting of these parameters provides important perceptions of safety and predictability so teens can function freely.

Principle 8: Be What You Want to See

Teenage Research Unlimited found that 70% of teenagers name their mom or dad as the person they most admire. Parents need to realize that who we are is much more important than what we say during these years. Teens, while unwilling to listen to our words of wisdom, learn volumes from observing us, even when we think they're not paying the remotest attention.

Principle 9: Let Go and Trust

Everyone hits rough patches in parenting, and they can occur almost daily during adolescence. But it is critical during these most trying of times to release our own feelings of shame, guilt, frustration, and pain and remember that we are in spiritual partnership with our teenagers. By letting go of the feelings of struggle, we can strengthen ourselves in the peace of trust, while still keeping a watchful eye.

Principle 10: Each Day Offers a Possibility of Renewal

Beginning anew usually means making small changes in the right direction; rather than quantum leaps toward a perfect relationship. It is truly the small day-to-day stuff that can shift a tense relationship with your teen: one thoughtful compliment a day, replacing irritation with understanding, or suggesting options rather than insisting upon specific solutions. Just when you've been counting the months until they leave the nest, suddenly a whole new direction takes root and you can enjoy your precious and rebellious teen.

The teenage brain is a work in progress, and society should realize this and show love and kindness. 1st Cor. 13:4 say, "Love endures long and is patient and kind; love never is envious nor boils over with jealousy, is not boastful or vainglorious, does not display itself haughtily." (Amplified Version) This scripture should be applied by teens, parents, and society. Remember, the adolescent years are full of growth conflicts. Immature choices and irrational decisions of adolescents are caused by the undeveloped mind which is still under construction.

Chapter 8

Teen Favorites

Top Five Websites Teen Visit

According to The Jamaica Observer, the top 5 websites teens visit are: Myspace, YouTube, hi5, Google, Wikipedia.

A survey by Wired.com Blog Network, Listening Post's states the hottest digital music websites are: Imeem, IVideoSongs, MOG, Muxtape, RCRD LBL, SeeqPod, Sellaband/SlicethePie, TuneCore, and YouTube.

Top Five Teen Magazines

According to All You Can Read.com, the top 5 teen magazines are: Teen, Cosmo Girl, Seventeen, Girl's Life Magazine, and Teen People.

Top Five cell phones Teens Want

According to Digg Del.icio.us Reddit Facebook Kent German, Senior Editor CNET (Sep 19, 2008) , the best 5 cell phones are: Apple iPhone 3G, RIM BlackBerry Curve 8320, Nokia N95, Samsung Instinct, Sony Ericsson W760i

Top Ivy League Colleges and Universities

Brown, Columbia, Cornell, Dartmouth, Harvard, Penn, Princeton and Yale

According to U.S. News Nation & World Health Money & Business Education (Opinion Science Photo Video Rankings Best Colleges 2009. Article Index Subscribe Home > Education > Best Colleges: Sunday, September 21, 2008). High School Counselor Rankings of National Universities: U.S.News asked guidance counselors from America's best high schools to tell them which national universities they think offer the best education to their students. The results are listed on colleges. usnews.rankingsandreviews.com/college/national-counselor-rank. Also the following article on U.S.News website is an excellent guide for students with average grades: A+ Option for B Students. If you're a good student with less than stellar test scores or so-so grade-point average, these are the lists for you. These colleges, which have strong *U.S. News* ratings, accept a significant number of students with nonstratospheric transcripts. http://colleges.usnews.rankingsandreviews.com/college/a-plus.

Conclusion

People say they don't understand why teenagers act the way they do. This book has been written to provide a better understanding of what teenagers' experience. Based on concrete evidence, MRI research of the adolescent brain gives us some answers to teen behavior.

Parts of the brain undergo refinement during the teen years. The adolescent brain still is strengthening connections between its reasoning and emotion-related regions. Adolescents are often unable to break their early emotional bonds logically. They may become rebellious emotionally, or hypercritical in order to persuade their parents that they are now different and must be independent. This behavior may breed alienation (the generation gap). Teenagers and adults often don't see eye to eye, but new brain research is explaining why. Although adolescence is often characterized by increased independence and a desire for knowledge and exploration, it is also a time when brain changes can result in high-risk behaviors, addictions, and mental illness, as different parts of the brain mature at different rates. Research has shown that cognitive control over high-risk behaviors is still maturing during adolescence, making teens more apt to engage in risky behaviors. Brain maturation is still going on well into adulthood. It takes more intense reward to stimulate a teen's brain. The brain's reward center, the ventral striatum, also is more active during adolescence than in adulthood, and the adolescent brain still is strengthening connections between its reasoning- and emotion-related regions. And that could lead some to take risks ranging from extreme sports to drinking or drugs.

As stated earlier, the most surprising thing about the teen brain is how much it is changing. By age six, the brain is already 95 percent of its adult size. In the frontal part of the brain, the part of the brain involved in judgment, organization, planning, strategizing (those very skills that teens get better and better at) this process of thickening of the gray matter peaks at about age 11 in girls and age 12 in boys, roughly about the same time as puberty.

Scientists once thought the brain's key development ended within the first few years of life. Scientists now can map brain tissue growth spurts and losses, allowing researchers to compare brain growth in both health and disease and to pinpoint where brain changes are most prominent in disease.

Many teens, for example, use adolescence as a time to experiment with drugs. Atypical brain changes and behaviors also can appear in adolescence. During adolescence, brain connections and signaling mechanisms selectively change over time to meet the needs of the environment.

Teens think with the amygdalae. That's the instinctual and emotional portion of the brain. The changes that take place in teen brains make teens want to take more risks and to seek higher and higher levels of stimulation. Teenagers are not adults. Teens are different from adults for some really basic physiological decisions. Their brains are simply different.

Rational decision making is a process for making logically sound decisions. Teen risk-taking is much higher than in adults - teenagers are more likely to abuse drugs and alcohol and take sexual risks - but the reasons for it are hotly debated. As a teenager moves into adulthood, there seems to be a shift in where the brain routes judgment calls—from the amygdalae (groups of neurons located deep within the medial temporal lobes) to the frontal lobe. Throw into this mix the abuse of alcohol or illegal drugs, or risky behavior in general, and it becomes even more difficult for the adolescent or young adult mind to fully appreciate the consequences of some choices.

Researchers found that the section of the brain associated with drive and motivation—the right ventral striatum—is far less developed in teens than in adults. The teen brain requires a lot more stimulation before anything registers.

The human brain contains a huge number of chemical synapses; young children have about 10 quadrillion synapses. This number declines with age, stabilizing by adulthood. As stated earlier research from the National Institutes of Health shows teen brains have extra synapses in the areas responsible for judging risks and making decisions. Many teenagers are in violent relationships where mental and physical abuse takes place. Today, some people are literally, "loving their partners to death". If one partner tries to break-up or leave the relationship, murder-suicide occurs. Teenagers can easily mistake sex for love, and having unprotected sex is risky business. 1 Corinthians 13:4-7 says, "Love is patient, love is kind. Love is an important factor in intimate relationships.

The complications of parent adolescent interaction are compounded by the adolescents striving for independence, by the increasing important of his/her peer group, and by changing social influences. Because of rapid social change, many contemporary adolescents, experiences fall outside of the range of parental understanding. Furthermore, many teens feel that his/her parents do not try to understand their problems. Both parents and adolescents bear responsibility for increasing their communications, although parents may have to initiate new activities and new forms of communications. Brain maturation is still going on well into adulthood. And as a parent, a parent's job will be to help transition to get to that point in adulthood. And that means giving kids your views and judgment to fall back on until they're ready to rely on their own.

Three influences become important to teenagers: sex, drugs, and motor vehicles. The need for love and acceptance, the influence of sexual hormones, and the sexual openness in our society, make sexual intercourse a common experience for adolescents. Adolescents are more likely to engage in high-risk behaviors, such as <u>unprotected sex</u>, when they are under the influence of drugs or alcohol. In 2005, 23% of high school students who had sexual intercourse during the past three months drank alcohol or used drugs before last sexual intercourse.

Teens feel a strong need to be intimate. Most people have several relationships throughout their lives, and most teens don't marry their first crush! For teens, romantic relationships can begin and get serious very quickly. The fact is that most teen relationships — even the strongest ones — usually end. According to CDC's Youth Risk Behavioral Survey (YRBS), many young people begin having sexual intercourse at early ages: 47% of high school students have had sexual intercourse, and 7.4% of them reported first sexual intercourse before age 13. HIV/AIDS education needs to take place at correspondingly young ages, before young people engage in sexual behaviors that put them at risk for HIV infection. Every year 1 in 4 sexually active teens contracts an STD. 81% of persons aged 15–24 70% of persons aged 13–14. Teen pregnancies carry extra health risks to the mother and the baby. They require special understanding because depression is also common among pregnant teens. The teenage mother has special problems, physically and emotionally.

You may be surprised to learn that young people do want to hear from parents and other adults about sex, love, and relationships. Show us why teen pregnancy is such a bad idea. Talk to us honestly about love, sex, and relationships. Tell us how you felt as a teen. Programs for teen moms and teen fathers are great, but we all need encouragement, attention, and support. Sex is serious. If you're drunk or high, you can't make good decisions about sex.

Adolescents and young adults often experience stress, confusion, and depression from situations occurring in their families, schools, and communities. Suicide is the third leading cause of death among young people ages 15 to 24. Suicide rates among older teen girls, those aged 15-19 shot up 32 percent; rates for males in that age group rose 9 percent. Many teens, unable to cope with family situations such as parents divorcing, having to live with step-parents and step-siblings, school, and low self-esteem are stressed, confused, and depressed. According to the American Academy of Child & Adolescent Psychiatry, depression and suicidal feelings are treatable mental disorders. Some symptoms are withdrawal from friends, family, and regular activities drug and alcohol use. Before the mid-1970s, suicide by adolescents appeared to be a rare event; now one out of ten teens contemplates suicide, and nearly a half million teens make a suicide attempt each year. Young adults are at a time when there are changes. Changes in relationships with parents, peers and others in society occur. The young adult stage involves the need to socialize and make new friends. Most young adults work while continuing their education.

Many teens are in abusive relationships. An abusive relationship is an interpersonal relationship characterized by the use or threat of physical or psychological abuse. Abusive relationships are often characterized by jealousy, emotional withholding, infidelity, sexual coercion, verbal abuse, broken promises, physical violence, control games and power plays. These relationships are often progressive. Abusive relationships can range from physical, emotional and sexual abuse. Adolescents and adults often don't make the link between dating abuse and poor health. Teens may remain in an abusive relationship for many reasons, including:

- self-blame
- Loyalty or love for the perpetrator
- Social stigma or peer pressure

Rates of drug, alcohol, and tobacco use are more than twice as high in girls who report physical or sexual dating abuse than in girls who report no abuse (Plichta 1996).

Dating abuse is associated with unhealthy sexual behaviors that can lead to unintended pregnancy, sexually-transmitted diseases, and HIV infections (Silverman et al. 2001).

Adolescents in abusive relationships often carry these unhealthy patterns of abuse into future relationships (Smith et al. 2003).

Dating abuse is defined as the physical, sexual, or psychological/emotional violence within a dating relationship. Each year, 1 in 11 adolescent's reports being a victim of physical dating abuse (CDC 2006). Abuse can be physical, sexual or emotional, which is the hardest to recognize. How do you know if a Friend Is Being Abused? A friend who is being abused needs your patience, love, and understanding.

Dating abuse can be prevented. Several studies suggest that adolescents do not see the negative consequences of dating abuse and violence in their friends' lives. Adolescents often believe that unhealthy relationships are the norm. If you can't love someone without feeling afraid, it's time to get out of the relationship now. Never isolate yourself from your friends and family.

Some teens are talking back to their parent's, some are verbally, emotional or physically abusive to their parents. Some teen are deliberately withholding communication from their parents, which is a form of control. Parents must have clear rules and consequences, and monitor the young person's whereabouts. Teens learn core values at home and church. Also, parents should never let teens show disrespectful. It is critical that parents never compromise on teens lying and being disrespectful because teens are in transition into adulthood and these are part of their core values. Teens must establish relationship boundaries with friends. Teens need to learn boundaries and self control when it comes to drinking.

Binge drinking impacts brain development, especially the younger the individual is. Teens should realize that today's choices create the future. Teaching teens about nutrition, grocery shopping, home management, beliefs about money, saving, banking & credit, and budgeting/spending plan will help them develop life-long skills.

Some teens steal from their parents, drink, have sex or do drugs in their parent's home. Some teens throw wild parties at home sometimes with their parents permission. Teens are incapable of making adult rational decisions because their brain is not fully developed yet, which explains why teens think and act the way they do. Many parents and church leaders fail to realize the intense pressures and problems facing teenagers today, which includes hormonal changes, sexual urges and the pressures to turn on with drugs and sex. Parents need to understand what it's like to be an adolescent in today's society. Being told to "grow up" can't make their brain mature any faster. Teens are under a lot more pressure and also must face many choices that their parents have never faced. Teens have to be cautious and make wise decisions, or risk becoming potential victims. The problem is that teens are trying to make adult decisions inside a child's mind, which explains why many teens feel rules and restrictions are unfair.

Teenage life consists of a multitude of emotional peaks and valleys. Teens experience growing pains such as awkward behavior, anger, and playing the blame game. Much of today's music, movies and teen magazines promote their ideas of an adult lifestyle. Many teens today are demanding money, and free leisure time away from home. Teen choices and parental responsibilities often clash, as teens say yes and parents say no not yet, causing anger, resentment, disappointment and uncertainty on both sides. If peer values are adopted, parental conflict may arise.

Teens are growing up listening both to parents and peers as they attempt to make independent decisions. Teens have a strong desire to be with their peers and some are resisting adult's rules; but at the same time, this is the time teens need adults the most to complete their transition into adulthood.

One of the factors contributing to the delinquency of teens is insufficient monitoring by parents after school. Adults can also help by making this point plain to their teens: Alcohol alters a person's ability to think clearly. Teens like to socialize and Teens love to attend parties to have a good time and socialize. Many teens drink and drive. To keep your teen safe from drinking and driving, one solution would be to install an Intoxalock ignition system in the teen's car. The result will be peace of mind for the parent and safety for the teen.

Communication is especially important during teen years. Teens are causing parents to alter the way they communicate to fit the growing needs of adolescents. To improve communications, one could turn off the television, avoid talking on the phone, and not read the newspaper if a teen wants to talk. Let your teen know that you are interested and that you will help when needed. Teens shouldn't be embarrassed in front of others. In a loving relationship, it is all about giving of oneself. Teens can't help who they are; they can't yet function like an adult's. This guide helps teens to develop an internal framework and moral compass to stay centered during turbulent years. Teens hunger to be a part of something.

Remember that teens typically struggle with a low self-image, at the same time that their need for love and acceptance is at an all time high. Loving words from a parent fuels a child, no matter their age. Teens simply want to be heard and respected.

By the time children reach their teen years, parents have gotten complacent about setting rules and creating family guidelines. The teenage brain is a work in progress, and society should realize this and show love and kindness. This scripture should be applied by teens, parents, and society. Remember, the adolescent years are full of growth conflicts. Now here is concrete evidence, based on MRI of the brain that gives us some answers to teen behavior. During the teen years, parts of the brain undergo changes. Planning and decision-making area of the brain, also, doesn't reach adult dimension until the early twenties. Some people wonder why older teenagers take such risk with their lives; brain changes can result in high-risk behaviors, and addictions, as different parts of the brain mature at different rates. A changing society, lack of moral standards, and an undeveloped teen mind, lead to conflicts with little solutions until the teen brain matures. Teens are incapable of making adult decisions and yet they sometimes are expected to think and act like adults. Teens are still growing up physically and mentally as the brain continues to grow.

Parents, never give up on your teens even when they are not doing what they know is right. Keep believing in them and keep them in your heart and prayers. Put God first in your life. A family that prays together stays together. We all make mistakes, fall short and need forgiveness. Parents must take the lead in forgiveness and acceptance even while we differ in our viewpoints. When parents are met with defiance and anger, who are we being in the face of denial, resistance and opposition? Are we being loving and kind or are we being critical and judgmental? Parental love and support binds and strengthens families. A house divided cannot stand, love one another right now. Make amends, ask for forgiveness and forgive each other. Families must stick together, together we stand divided we fall.

Our civilization is fixated with happy endings and believes that getting married can fix anything. Just look at "reality" shows like *The Bachelor* and *Joe Millionaire* and movies like *Maid in Manhattan* and *Just Married*. Their message is that getting married is for a lifetime and turns life into a fairy tale which is dangerous because fairy tales have nothing to do with reality. The key word here is lifetime and that's a very long time, making the commitment a very serious decision. For teens, romantic relationships can begin and get serious very quickly. We think they will last forever. But they rarely do. Many people enjoy being in a relationship, but that doesn't mean that it's going to last forever or that it should. The fact is that most teen relationships even the strongest ones usually end. If a person is truly in love, that love will still be there waiting when they are ready and mature enough to deal with the problems and issues of marriage.

We, the authors, have experience rearing teenagers and understand the tremendous challenges teens face. Yes, we've been through turmoil with our teens, but we supported and guided them through those tough times. We sincerely hope this book will alleviate some of the pressures of rearing teens and help your teen make a smoother transition into adulthood.

Work Cited

American Academy of Pediatrics

Anderson RN, Smith BL. Deaths: leading causes for 2001. National Vital Statistics Report 2003; 52(9):1-86.

Centers for Disease Control and Prevention. Regional variations in suicide rates—United States 1990–1994, August 29, 1997. MMWR 1997; 46(34):789-92.

Ackard DM, Neumark-Sztainer D. Date violence and date rape among adolescents: associations with disordered eating behaviors and psychological health. Child Abuse and Neglect 2002; 26:455–73.

Arriaga XB, Foshee VA. Adolescent dating violence. Do adolescents follow in their friends' or their parents' footsteps? Journal of Interpersonal Violence 2004; 19(2):162–84.

Avery-Leaf S, Cascardi M, O'Leary KD, Cano A. Efficacy of a dating violence prevention program on attitudes justifying aggression. Journal of Adolescent Health 1997;21:11–7.

Bergman, L. Dating violence among high school students. Social Work 1992;37:21–7.

Centers for Disease Control and Prevention. Physical dating violence among high school students — United States, 2003. MMWR 2006; 55:532-535.

Feiring C, Furman WC. When love is just a four-letter word: victimization and romantic relationships in adolescence. Child Maltreatment 2000;5(4):293–8.

Foshee VA, Bauman KE, Ennett ST, Suchindran C, Benefield T, Linder FG. Assessing the effects of the dating violence prevention program "Safe Dates" using random coefficient regression modeling. Prevention Science 2005;6(3):245–58.

Foshee VA, Linder GF, Bauman KE, et al. The Safe Dates Project: theoretical basis, evaluation design, and selected baseline findings. American Journal of Preventive Medicine 1996;12(2):39–47.

Halpern CT, Oslak SG, Young ML, Martin SL, Kupper LL. Partner violence among adolescents in opposite-sex romantic relationships: findings from the National Longitudinal Study of Adolescent Health. American Journal of Public Health 2001;91(10):1679–85.

Hotaling GT, Sugarman DB. An analysis of risk markers in husband to wife violence: the current state of knowledge. Violence and Victims 1986;1(2):101–24.

Jaffe P, Sudermann M, Reitzel D, Killip S. An evaluation of a secondary school primary prevention program on violence in intimate relationships. Violence and Victims 1992;7:129–46.

Plichta SB. Violence and abuse: implications for women's health. In: Falik MM, Collins KS, editors. Women's health: the commonwealth survey. Baltimore (MD): Johns Hopkins University Press; 1996.

Silverman JG, Raj A, Mucci L, Hathaway J. Dating violence against adolescent girls and associated substance use, unhealthy weight control, sexual risk behavior, pregnancy, and suicidality. Journal American Medical Association 2001;286(5):572–9.

Smith PH, White JW, Holland LJ. A longitudinal perspective on dating violence among adolescent and college-age women. American Journal of Public Health 2003;93(7):1104–9.

Wekerle C, Wolfe DA. Dating violence in mid-adolescence: theory, significance, and emerging prevention initiatives. Clinical Psychological Review 1999;19:435–56.

Wolfe DA, Wekerle C, Scott K. Alternatives to violence: empowering youth to develop health relationships. Thousand Oaks (CA): Sage; 1997.

http://www.hartfordinstitute.org/research/religion_family.html
Lindsay, Jeanne Warren. *Caring, Commitment and Change*. Morning Glory Press, Inc., 1995.

Ponton, Lynn (2000). *The Sex Lives of Teenagers*. New York: Dutton, 2. ISBN 0452282608.

The Timing of Normal Puberty and the Age Limits of Sexual Precocity: Variations around the World, Secular Trends, and Changes after Migration.

Ponton, Lynn (2000). *The Sex Lives of Teenagers*. New York: Dutton, 3. ISBN 0452282608.

Dr. Liz Alderman, an adolescent medicine specialist at Montefiore Medical Center

Teenage Brain Development By Jennifer Lang, MS, LMFT

Inside the Teen Brain, U.S. News & World Report, August 9, 1999 Getting Inside a Teen Brain, Newsweek

Current Directions in Psychological Science. 2000 Feb Vol 9(1) 26-29. Aggressive Behavior. 1998 Vol 24(6) 421-438. Journal of Personality & Social Psychology. 1998 Jul Vol 75(1) 219-229.

© 2003-2007 Vertical Thought — a magazine of understanding for tomorrow's leaders

Frontline: Inside the teen brain; Interview Jay Giedd

Credit: J. Geoff Malta, MA, EdM, NCC Adolescent Therapist Puberty 101 Archives

www.**niace.org.uk**/information/Briefing_sheets/**Young_ Adults**_MHD.htm

willpower.4mg.com/whatislove.html

Christian Counseling, A Comprehensive Guide, Gary R. Collins

(Bergen 1996; Coker et al. 2002; Heise and Garcia-Moreno 2002; Roberts, Klein, and Fisher 2003):

Society for Neuroscience January 2007
Source: Professor Hossein Arsham, University of Baltimore
Dan Kurland's www.criticalreading.com
Reading and Writing Ideas As Well As Words (rational thinking)
Source: www.coolnurse.com
"Brain immaturity can be deadly" by Elizabeth Williamson MSNBC | February 1, 2005

National Campaign to Prevent Teen and Unplanned Pregnancy

Tough Love Solutions
Phyllis York, David York, and Ted Wachtel

http://www.parkridge.k12.nj.us/AYeager/Tips_for_Parents.htm